Floristic Inventory of Bluestone National Scenic River, West Virginia

Technical Report NPS/NER/NRTR—2008/105

Brian P. Streets, James P. Vanderhorst, Celeste Good, and Greg Short

WV Natural Heritage Program
Wildlife Resource Section
West Virginia Division of Natural Resources
P.O. Box 67
Elkins, WV 26241

July 2008

U.S. Department of the Interior
National Park Service
Northeast Region
Philadelphia, Pennsylvania

The Northeast Region of the National Park Service (NPS) comprises national parks and related areas in 13 New England and Mid-Atlantic states. The diversity of parks and their resources are reflected in their designations as national parks, seashores, historic sites, recreation areas, military parks, monuments and memorials, and rivers and trails. Biological, physical, and social science research results, natural resource inventory and monitoring data, scientific literature reviews, bibliographies, and proceedings of technical workshops and conferences related to these park units are disseminated through the NPS/NER Technical Report (NRTR) and Natural Resources Report (NRR) series. The reports are a continuation of series with previous acronyms of NPS/PHSO, NPS/MAR, NPS/BSO-RNR, and NPS/NERBOST. Individual parks may also disseminate information through their own report series.

Natural Resources Reports are the designated medium for information on technologies and resource management methods; "how to" resource management papers; proceedings of resource management workshops or conferences; and natural resource program descriptions and resource action plans.

Technical Reports are the designated medium for initially disseminating data and results of biological, physical, and social science research that addresses natural resource management issues; natural resource inventories and monitoring activities; scientific literature reviews; bibliographies; and peer-reviewed proceedings of technical workshops, conferences, or symposia.

Mention of trade names or commercial products does not constitute endorsement or recommendation for use by the National Park Service.

This report was accomplished under Cooperative Agreement H4560-05-0001, with assistance from the NPS. The statements, findings, conclusions, recommendations, and data in this report are solely those of the author(s), and do not necessarily reflect the views of the U.S. Department of the Interior, National Park Service.

Print copies of reports in these series, produced in limited quantity and only available as long as the supply lasts, or preferably, file copies on CD, may be obtained by sending a request to the address on the back cover. Print copies also may be requested from the NPS Technical Information Center (TIC), Denver Service Center, PO Box 25287, Denver, CO 80225-0287. A copy charge may be involved. To order from TIC, refer to document D-009A.

This report may also be available as a downloadable portable document format file from the Internet at http://www.nps.gov/nero/science/.

Please cite this publication as:

Streets B. P., J. P. Vanderhorst, C. Good, and G. Short. 2008. Floristic Inventory of Bluestone National Scenic River, West Virginia. Technical Report NPS/NER/NRTR—2008/105. National Park Service. Philadelphia, PA.

NPS D-009A July 2008

Table of Contents

	Page
Tables	v
Figures	vii
Appendixes	ix
Acknowledgments	xi
Executive Summary	xiii
Introduction	1
Study Area	3
Methods	7
Review of Existing Data	7
Floristic Inventory	7
Rare, Threatened, and Endangered Plant Surveys	9
Annotated Checklist	9
Results	11
Review of Existing Data	11
Floristic Inventory	13
Rare, Threatened, and Endangered Plant Species	14
Floristic Summary	14
Discussion and Management Recommendations	19
Literature Cited	23

Tables

Page

Table 1. Plant taxa collected in the vicinity outside the boundary (with precise location data) and in the vicinity of the boundary (with imprecise location data) of Bluestone National Scenic River. 15

Table 2. Element Occurrence Records (EORs) of rare, threatened, and endangered plant species in Bluestone National Scenic River entered in the Biotics database as of May 31, 2007. 16

Figures

Page

Figure 1. Bluestone National Scenic River, West Virginia, and vicinity. 4

Figure 2. Locations of walk-through survey plant collection sites and vegetation plots in Bluestone National Scenic River, 2003–2006. 8

Figure 3. Photograph of butternut (*Juglans cinerea*) taken in the gorge of Indian Branch, Bluestone National Scenic River, on April 24, 2004. 20

Appendixes

Page

Appendix A. State and global conservation rank and federal threatened
and endangered status definitions. 27

Appendix B. Annotated checklist of vascular plants known from
Bluestone National Scenic River, West Virginia. 31

Appendix C. Definitions of plant nativity status. 77

Appendix D. Definitions of invasive ranks. 79

Appendix E. Definitions of estimated abundance ranks. 81

Acknowledgments

We would like to thank the following individuals for their help with this project. Ken Stephens, John Perez, and Beth Johnson (National Park Service) assisted with contracting and logistics. Tom Vogt (Abies Ecology) assisted with field work in 2003. Dr. Robert Naczi identified several collections of *Carex* and provided access to the herbarium at Delaware State University. Dr. Donna Ford-Werntz provided access to the herbarium at West Virginia University and Dr. Tonya McKinley provided access to the herbarium at Concord University. Dr. James Rentch (West Virginia University) provided unpublished data from vegetation plots in the park. Elizabeth Byers and Barbara Sargent (WV Natural Heritage Program) assisted with Biotics.

Executive Summary

A floristic inventory of Bluestone National Scenic River, located in southern West Virginia, was conducted from 2003 to 2006 by the West Virginia Natural Heritage Program. Prior to field work, literature and databases were reviewed to compile a list of vascular plants already known to occur in Bluestone National Scenic River. Six hundred sixty-eight vascular plant taxa were identified during the 2003–2006 field surveys including 367 taxa not previously documented from the study area. The documented flora of Bluestone National Scenic River now consists of 786 taxa representing 762 species (some with multiple subspecies or varieties) in 116 plant families. Six hundred eighty taxa (86% of the flora) are native to West Virginia, seven taxa (0.9%) are introduced, 99 taxa (13%) are exotic, one taxon (0.1%) is adventive, and one taxon (0.1%) is of unknown origin. Seventy-seven taxa are listed as invasive in West Virginia. Thirty-nine taxa are tracked as rare, threatened, or endangered in West Virginia, nine of which are considered globally rare. One occurrence of the federally listed threatened Virginia meadowsweet (*Spiraea virginiana*) is known from the park. Six hundred twenty-one taxa (79% of the known flora) are represented by known collections from the park. Eighteen collections from the 2003–2006 surveys are considered Mercer County records and 31 are considered Summers County records. Collections of two species, rusty blackhaw (*Viburnum rufidulum*) and quill sedge (*Carex tenera*), are possible state records.

Introduction

The National Park Service (NPS) Inventory and Monitoring (I&M) Program has established a goal to document 90% of the estimated species of vertebrates and vascular plants which occur in national parks that contain significant natural resources (NPS 1999). Authoritative documentation of the occurrence of vascular plants is best established by collections of voucher specimens. Another goal of the I&M Program is to document the distribution and abundance of species of special concern, including threatened, endangered, and other globally or state rare species. Methods and databases developed by NatureServe and the network of Natural Heritage Programs are designed for documenting occurrences of species of special concern. A scoping meeting held in Glen Jean, WV, in 2000, hosted by the I&M Program and attended by West Virginia natural scientists, identified a floristic inventory of Bluestone National Scenic River (BLUE) as one of the inventory priorities for the West Virginia national parks located in the NPS Eastern Rivers and Mountains Network (NPS 2000). In 2003, a floristic inventory, including surveys for vascular plant species of special concern, was funded by the NPS to be conducted in concurrence with vegetation classification and mapping for the park.

The floristic inventory for BLUE was completed by the West Virginia Natural Heritage Program (WVNHP), part of the Wildlife Resources Section of the Division of Natural Resources. WVNHP conducts inventories and maintains databases of the natural biological diversity of the state, including natural ecological communities and rare, threatened, and endangered plants and animals. WVNHP is part of a network including programs from each of the 50 United States, all Provinces of Canada, and several Latin American countries, with the non-profit organization NatureServe acting as network coordinator. NatureServe and the network of Natural Heritage Programs are the leading source of detailed information on biological diversity in the Americas.

Data on the taxonomy, biology, and distribution of natural ecological communities and rare, threatened, and endangered animal and plant species is maintained in Biotics (NatureServe 2007a; WVDNR 2007), a georeferenced database developed and maintained by NatureServe and the network of Natural Heritage Programs. In Biotics, natural ecological communities and rare, threatened, and endangered species are known as Elements (NatureServe 2002). The area of land where the Element is or was known to occur is the Element Occurrence (EO). The record of the occurrence stored in Biotics is the Element Occurrence Record (EOR). Biotics utilizes both spatial and tabular data to document these occurrences. NatureServe assigns global conservation ranks for federally and state listed rare, threatened, and endangered species. Global ranks are based on worldwide occurrence and distribution information, including data obtained from state Natural Heritage Programs. WVNHP maintains a list of rare, threatened, and endangered plants in West Virginia and assigns state conservation ranks for taxa based on documented occurrences within the state (WVNHP 2007). WVNHP also assigns Element Occurrence ranks which estimate the relative viability of individual EOs (NatureServe 2002). Federal threatened and endangered status is determined by the U. S. Fish and Wildlife Service (USFWS) based on criteria set forth by the Endangered Species Act (USFWS 1973). Definitions for state ranks, global ranks, and federal threatened and endangered status are provided in Appendix A.

This project was undertaken to provide information to improve the protection and management of the plant resources of BLUE. The primary objectives of this study were to 1) document the vascular plant diversity of the park, 2) contribute specimens to the NPS reference herbarium in Glen Jean, WV, and to the West Virginia University Herbarium in Morgantown, WV, and 3) survey and document occurrences of rare, threatened, and endangered plant species found within the park. This information will help assess global and regional plant species distributions and abundances, identify management priorities, and serve as a baseline for establishment of monitoring programs for the park.

Study Area

The Bluestone National Scenic River (BLUE) is centered on a 17-km (10.5-mi) stretch of the Bluestone River which flows through a relatively unspoiled section of northeastern Mercer and southwestern Summers counties in southern West Virginia (Figure 1). The park begins approximately 3 km (1.8 mi) upstream from the mouth of Mountain Creek and follows the Bluestone River downstream to the boundary of Bluestone State Park. The proclamation boundary of the park encompasses approximately 1,755 ha (4,337 ac) mapped on the Flat Top and Pipestem 1:24,000 USGS quadrangles. BLUE was established as a National Park Service unit on October 26, 1988, when it was created from sections of Pipestem State Park, Bluestone State Park, and a portion of the Bluestone Wildlife Management Area. It is managed by the New River Gorge National River office in Glen Jean, WV.

The park encompasses much of the inner Bluestone River gorge, most of Pilot Ridge, 2 km (1.2 mi) of the lower section of the Little Bluestone River, and a few smaller named tributaries including Indian Branch, Mountain Creek, and Tony Hollow. The park includes the Bluestone River and its tributaries and shores, small areas of alluvial floodplains, large areas of moderate to steep gorge slopes, and a few narrow ridge tops. Elevations in the park range from 435 m (1,429 ft) along the Bluestone River at the northern boundary to 730 m (2,389 ft) along the boundary on a ridge north of Tony Hollow.

Ecoregional assignment of the park is highly variable depending on which mapping system is used. The Environmental Protection Agency (Woods et al. 2003) includes the park within the Dissected Appalachian Plateau Level III Ecoregion within the Central Appalachian Level IV Ecoregion. The United States Forest Service (Bailey et al. 1994) places the park within the Northern Cumberland Mountains Section of the Central Appalachian Broad Leaf Forest – Coniferous Forest – Meadow Province. The Nature Conservancy (Sotomayor 2004) places the park within the Central Appalachian Forest Ecoregion.

The climate of the park is a humid continental type characterized by marked seasonal temperature changes and relatively uniform precipitation throughout the year. Mean monthly temperatures at nearby Bluestone Lake (elevation 423 m [1,390 ft]) range from -0.44°C (31.2°F) in January to 22.9°C (73.3°F) in July (NOAA 2002). Normal annual precipitation at Bluestone Lake is 95.8 cm (37.72 in) and monthly precipitation ranges from 6.4 cm (2.52 in) in October to 10.6 cm (4.19 in) in July (NOAA 2002).

The bedrock geology of the park is mapped as Hinton, Bluestone, and Princeton formations of the Mauch Chunk Group (Cardwell et al. 1968). These Mississippian-aged formations consist primarily of shale and siltstone with lesser amounts of sandstone and limestone. The older Hinton formation is the predominant formation in the park and forms the valley floor and most gorge slopes. The Hinton formation includes partly calcareous shales and siltstones and the Stony Gap Member of the Avis Limestone (Englund et al. 1977; Englund et al. 1982). Smaller areas of the younger Bluestone and Princeton formations outcrop on the upper gorge slopes and plateaus of the park.

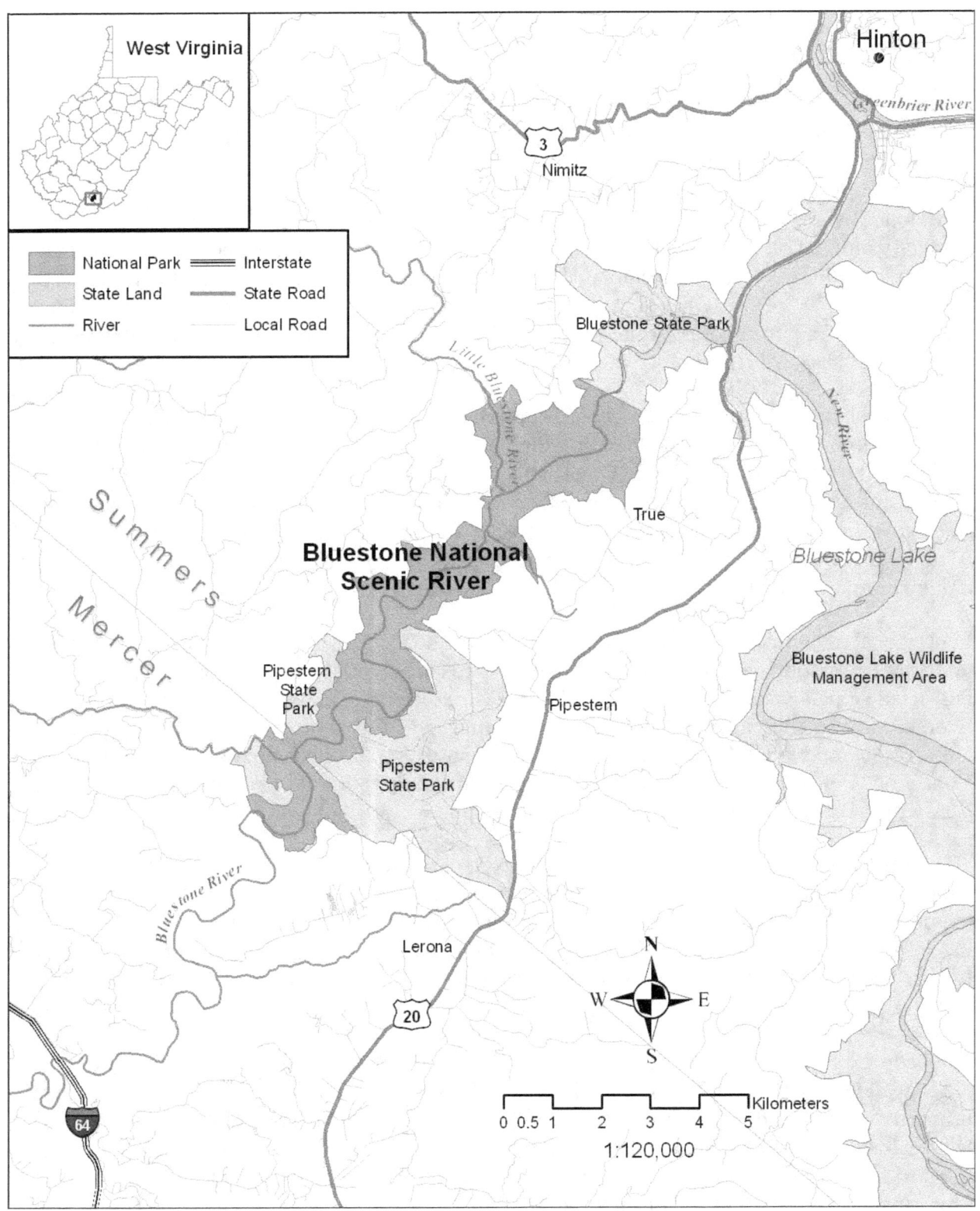

Figure 1. Bluestone National Scenic River, West Virginia, and vicinity.

Soils within the park are mapped as the Calvin high base substratum – Berks – Gilpin association and are described as moderately deep, strongly sloping to very steep, well-drained, lime-influenced and acidic soils (Sponaugle et al. 1984). Three major soil series are mapped here. The Calvin series is made up of moderately deep, well-drained soils formed in weathered acidic and lime-influenced shales, siltstones, and sandstones. The Berks series and the Gilpin series are made up of moderately deep, well-drained soils formed in weathered acidic shales, siltstones, and sandstones. Minor soil series occurring in the park include the Coolville, Dekalb, Latham, Lily, and Tilsit series on uplands, the Ernest, Jefferson, and Shouns series on footslopes, and the Orrville series on floodplains (Sponaugle et al. 1984).

The park is included within the mixed mesophytic region of the eastern deciduous forest biome (Braun 1950). The vegetation of the park is characterized by extensive upland deciduous forests and mixed conifer/deciduous forests with smaller areas of floodplain forests and riparian communities. Common upland trees include red maple (*Acer rubrum* var. *rubrum*), sugar maple (*Acer saccharum* var. *saccharum*), yellow buckeye (*Aesculus flava*), mockernut hickory (*Carya alba*), pignut hickory (*Carya glabra*), shagbark hickory (*Carya ovata*), white ash (*Fraxinus americana*), tuliptree (*Liriodendron tulipifera*), blackgum (*Nyssa sylvatica*), sourwood (*Oxydendrum arboreum*), eastern white pine (*Pinus strobus*), white oak (*Quercus alba*), scarlet oak (*Quercus coccinea* var. *coccinea*), chestnut oak (*Quercus prinus*), northern red oak (*Quercus rubra*), black oak (*Quercus velutina*), American basswood (*Tilia americana*), and eastern hemlock (*Tsuga canadensis*). Additional tree species common on floodplains include boxelder (*Acer negundo* var. *negundo*), river birch (*Betula nigra*), bitternut hickory (*Carya cordiformis*), green ash (*Fraxinus pennsylvanica*), black walnut (*Juglans nigra*), and American sycamore (*Platanus occidentalis*).

Previous botanical studies of BLUE include floristic inventories, surveys for rare, threatened, and endangered plants, and a study of vegetation patterns. Oxley (1975) completed a floristic inventory of the Indian Branch Gorge of Pipestem State Park. His study area is located entirely within the current NPS proclamation boundary. Norris (1992) surveyed and mapped locations of rare, threatened, and endangered plants and animals in BLUE. Grafton (1993) established two transects to compare vegetation occurring on moist and dry sites on the lower sections of the Bluestone River within the park. Fortney et al. (1994) completed a reconnaissance vegetation study of the Bluestone, New, and Gauley river gorges for the NPS. A transect was established within each national park. The Bluestone Gorge transect was located just north of the Pipestem State Park Tramway. Rentch et al. (2005) sampled vegetation plots both inside and outside the park boundaries to describe vegetation patterns of the lower Bluestone River Gorge.

Methods

Review of Existing Data

Prior to field work, literature and databases were reviewed to assemble a list of vascular plant taxa previously documented from BLUE. Five research projects, Oxley (1975), Norris (1992), Grafton (1993), Fortney et al. (1994), and Rentch et al. (2005), have documented vascular plant taxa known to occur at BLUE. The Biotics database (WVDNR 2007) was queried to determine occurrences of rare, threatened, or endangered plant taxa known from BLUE. NPSpecies (NPS 2003), the National Park Service's database for documenting the occurrence of species in national park units, was queried to determine known plant collections from the park. A limited number of plant collections from BLUE at the herbaria of West Virginia University in Morgantown, WV, and Concord University in Athens, WV, were examined, and misidentified specimens were annotated by the second author.

Floristic Inventory

A systematic, collection-based floristic inventory of the park began during the spring of 2003 and continued through the summer of 2006. Walk-through surveys were conducted throughout each of the growing seasons to thoroughly represent seasonal variation, ecological diversity, and the geographical range of the park. A running checklist of plants identified from the study area was created and updated during each field visit. The project goal was to collect two diagnostic voucher specimens for each vascular plant taxon found in the park, one for the NPS herbarium in Glen Jean, WV, and the second for the West Virginia University herbarium in Morgantown, WV. Additional duplicate collections were made of numerous taxa which were difficult to identify in the field. All duplicate collections were donated to West Virginia University herbarium. Collection was constrained by ethical collection guidelines set by The Plant Conservation Roundtable (1986) to avoid significant impacts to populations of rare, threatened, and endangered plants. Diagnostic reproductive material was collected whenever possible. Plant material was collected in plastic bags in the field and promptly pressed and dried. Field notes for collection sites included plant name, location (driving directions and either corrected GPS or hand-mapped coordinates), slope, aspect, elevation, habitat, associated species, collector(s), and collection date.

In addition to the floristic surveys, considerable floristic information was gathered while sampling plots for vegetation classification and mapping of BLUE (Vanderhorst et al., 2008). An attempt was made to identify and estimate abundance of all vascular plant taxa occurring in 400 m^2 (4,305 ft^2) vegetation plots. One hundred thirty-five plots were sampled during 2003–2005. Many of the collections for the floristic inventory of BLUE were made from plots and the plots represent a larger number of georeferenced observation records for plant taxa. Plot data included environmental comments, landscape comments, slope, aspect, elevation, and information on geology, landform, topographic position, hydrology, and soils. Locational coordinates for 119 vegetation plots, and collections from 16 sites outside of plots, were determined using Trimble or Garmin GPS units. Sites without GPS coordinates were mapped by hand on USGS topographic maps. All collection sites and vegetation plots were mapped using ESRI ArcGIS software (Figure 2).

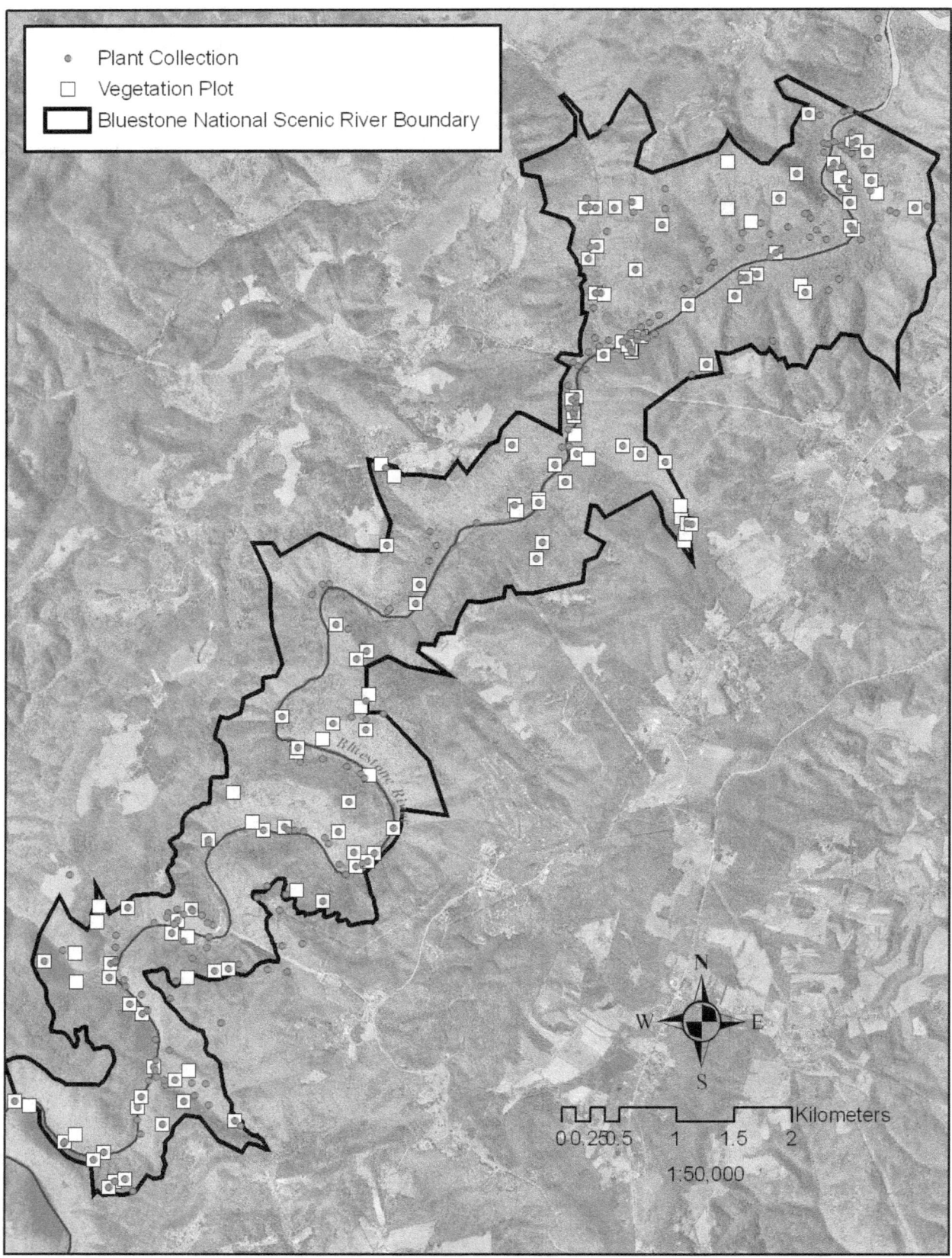

Figure 2. Locations of walk-through survey plant collection sites and vegetation plots in Bluestone National Scenic River, 2003–2006.

Preliminary identifications of most plants were made in the field using The Flora of West Virginia, 2nd ed. (Strausbaugh and Core 1977) and the Manual of Vascular Plants of Northeastern United States and Canada, 2nd ed. (Gleason and Cronquist 1991). All collections were also examined and keyed in the herbarium to verify or revise field determinations. Additional floristic references consulted in the herbarium include The Flora of the Carolinas, Virginia, Georgia, and Surrounding Area (Weakley 2006), The Plants of Pennsylvania (Rhoads and Block 2000), Plant Life of Kentucky (Jones 2005), and all pertinent volumes of the Flora of North America (Flora of North America Committee 1993+).

Identifications of *Carex* specimens were completed using the Flora of North America, Vol. 23 (Ball and Reznicek 2002). Some *Carex* collections were taken to Delaware State University and annotated by Dr. Robert Naczi, a specialist in the genus. Identifications of *Dichanthelium* specimens were completed using the Flora of North America, Vol. 25 (Freckmann and Lelong 2003). Collections of *Desmodium* were identified using a vegetative key developed by Krings (2004). *Heuchera* determinations were made using the Key to *Heuchera* in West Virginia (Norris 1999). *Monarda* specimens were determined using The Flora of the Carolinas, Virginia, Georgia, and Surrounding Area (Weakley 2006).

Herbarium labels were created for all plant collections using Theo, a Microsoft Access database developed by the New York Natural Heritage Program (Gebaur et al. 2002). Label data includes county, scientific name, plant family, common name, location (map directions and UTM coordinates), elevation, habitat, associated plants, collector's name, collection date, and determiner's name when different from the collector. One representative specimen of each vascular plant taxon collected was mounted on acid-free, museum-quality mounting paper and deposited in the NPS herbarium in Glen Jean, WV. All other collections were submitted unmounted with labels to the herbarium of West Virginia University in Morgantown, WV.

Rare, Threatened, and Endangered Plant Surveys

Rare, threatened, and endangered status was determined according to the most up-to-date (as of May 31, 2007) version of the list maintained by WVNHP (2007). When populations of listed plants were encountered, the area was surveyed and field forms filled out to record information including population (size, number of individuals, and phenology), location (driving directions and either corrected GPS or hand mapped coordinates), and environmental data (slope, aspect, elevation, habitat, and associated species). Locational data for each rare, threatened, or endangered plant Element Occurrence were entered in Biotics Mapper, and tabular data on each rare, threatened, or endangered plant Element Occurrence were entered in Biotics Tracker. Element Occurrence Records existing in Biotics prior to this study were updated with information gained during the 2003–2006 surveys. The Biotics database is maintained by WVNHP and exchanged with the central Biotics database maintained by NatureServe.

Annotated Checklist

An annotated checklist of vascular plants documented from BLUE (Appendix B) was produced using a Microsoft Access database. The checklist is a compilation of the literature review, database queries, herbarium investigations, and field data. Data entered includes plant family, scientific name, common name, plant nativity, invasive status, estimated abundance, whether it is listed as rare, threatened, or endangered and, if it is, state and global ranks and federal status (WVNHP 2007), collector(s) and collection numbers, whether a 2003–2006 collection is a county or state record, whether it occurred in a vegetation plot sampled during 2003–2006, and other studies in which it was documented from BLUE.

Names used in this report and associated databases follow the Checklist and Atlas of the Vascular Flora of West Virginia (Harmon et al. 2006), except in the cases of *Carex* and *Dichanthelium*, where the nomenclature was based on the Flora of North America (1993+). Due to changes in taxonomic concepts and nomenclature over time and disagreement among botanists, many of the names used by sources for this project (reports, publications, databases, and herbarium specimens) do not correspond to the accepted names used in this report. An attempt was made to translate these names to our accepted names without making assumptions which might misrepresent taxonomic determinations.

Collections of taxa that were not known from West Virginia prior to the 2003–2006 BLUE floristic surveys are considered state records. Collections of taxa that were not previously known from Summers and/or Mercer counties are considered county records. Taxa not previously known from Mercer and/or Summers counties that were identified but not collected during the 2003–2006 surveys are considered "potential" county records. Known state and county distributions prior to the 2003–2006 BLUE floristic surveys were determined according to the Checklist and Atlas of the Vascular Flora of West Virginia (Harmon et al. 2006). The checklist is a collection of county-based dot maps showing distribution of vascular plants based on vouchered herbarium specimens.

Nativity is a representation of a species' likelihood of occurrence in West Virginia prior to European settlement. Nativity was ascertained from the Checklist and Atlas of the Vascular Flora of West Virginia (Harmon et al. 2006). A list of nativity categories and their definitions is provided in Appendix C.

Invasive status within the state was determined using the Checklist of Invasive Plant Species of West Virginia (Harmon 2007). Invasive plants are species which tend to encroach into natural ecosystems in which they are not native and represent a possible threat to native plants in these habitats. A list of invasive categories and their definitions is provided in Appendix D.

Abundance of each taxon was estimated by the senior author depending on the number of occurrences and their geographical distribution based on ranks used by NPSpecies (Wotawa 2004). Definitions of abundance ranks are provided in Appendix E.

Results

Review of Existing Data

Oxley (1975) identified 293 taxa of vascular plants during his floristic survey of Indian Branch Gorge. Nine of these taxa are listed as rare, threatened, or endangered by WVNHP (2007): American barberry (*Berberis canadensis*), lip fern (*Cheilanthes tomentosa*), lesser rattlesnake plantain (*Goodyera repens*), sweet Indian plantain (*Hasteola suaveolens*), smooth sunflower (*Helianthus laevigatus*), fly honeysuckle (*Lonicera canadensis*), southern loosestrife (*Lysimachia tonsa*), cursed crowfoot (*Ranunculus sceleratus* var. *sceleratus*), and American yew (*Taxus canadensis*). Of these, only *Berberis canadensis* and *Lonicera canadensis* were observed during the 2003–2006 floristic surveys conducted by the WVNHP. A query of Biotics (WVDNR 2007) revealed that the only Element Occurrence Record based on the Oxley report entered prior to this project was the record for *Lysimachia tonsa*. Examination of the Oxley collections at Concord University by the second author revealed that specimens labeled as *Cheilanthes tomentosa* and *Ranunculus sceleratus* were misidentified. The Oxley specimen identified as *Cheilanthes tomentosa* was annotated as *Cheilanthes lanosa*, a relatively common species. The Oxley collection identified as *Ranunculus sceleratus* was annotated as *Ranunculus hispidus*, also a relatively common species. Based on these annotations, *Cheilanthes tomentosa* and *Ranunculus sceleratus* var. *sceleratus* were not included in the annotated checklist (Appendix B). We entered Element Occurrence Records in Biotics for the other six rare taxa documented by Oxley, although voucher specimens could not be found at Concord University herbarium for any of these except *Taxus canadensis*. Oxley's determinations for some of these may also have been incorrect.

In addition, Oxley (1975) identified four species not listed in the Checklist and Atlas of the Vascular Flora of West Virginia (Harmon et al. 2006) and which do not have WV distributions listed in NatureServe Explorer (NatureServe 2007b), USDA Plants (USDA, NRCS 2007), or the Flora of North America (FNA editorial committee 1993+). Greater burdock (*Arctium lappa*) is an exotic found in several adjacent states and could possibly occur in West Virginia. Spotted beebalm (*Monarda punctata*) occurs in all the adjacent states so it is possible that it could occur in West Virginia. Schweinitz's ragwort (*Packera schweinitziana*) is a northeastern species with a disjunct distribution at high elevations around Roan Mountain in North Carolina and Tennessee; its occurrence at the relatively low elevation of BLUE seems unlikely. Slender bulrush (*Schoenoplectus heterochaetus*) is listed as SH (possibly extirpated) in Kentucky and SX (presumed extirpated) in Pennsylvania but is not known from other adjacent states (NatureServe 2007b). The herbarium at Concord University was searched for the Oxley collections of these four taxa, but none were found. Due to the lack of voucher specimens to confirm determinations for these taxa, which would represent West Virginia state records, they were not included in the annotated checklist for BLUE (Appendix B).

Four additional Oxley specimens at Concord University examined by the second author were found to be misidentified. A specimen (Oxley collection # 15) labeled as deeproot clubmoss (*Lycopodium tristachyum*) was annotated as *Lycopodium digitatum*. *Lycopodium tristachyum* was included in the checklist (Appendix B) because it was listed by Rentch et al. (2005), but no specimens are known. A specimen (Oxley collection # 34) labeled as spinulose woodfern

(*Dryopteris spinulosa,* syn. *D. carthusiana*) was annotated as intermediate woodfern (*Dryopteris intermedia*). A specimen (Oxley collection # 1120) labeled as minniebush (*Menziesia pilosa*) was annotated as Blue Ridge blueberry (*Vaccinium pallidum*). A specimen (Oxley collection # 93) labeled as winter vetch (*Vicia villosa*) was annotated as veiny pea (*Lathyrus venosus*). Based on these annotations, *Dryopteris carthusiana, Menziesia pilosa,* and *Vicia villosa* were not included in the annotated checklist (Appendix B).

Although a systematic search of the herbarium at Concord University for collections from BLUE was not conducted, four additional collections were encountered by chance during our review of Oxley specimens there. These include two specimens of meadow spikemoss (*Selaginella apoda*) collected by C. J. Chapman (Concord accession #s 156 and 511), one collection of *Selaginella apoda* collected by B. Harris (Concord accession # 158), and one collection of shining clubmoss (*Huperzia lucidula*) collected by B. Harris (Concord accession # 145). All of these were collected from Indian Branch in the autumn of 1974 and had also been reported by Oxley (1975).

Norris (1992) identified 91 taxa of vascular plants during his survey of BLUE. Fifteen of these species are considered rare, threatened, or endangered and are tracked by WVNHP (2007): smallfruit agrimony (*Agrimonia microcarpa*), Lillydale onion (*Allium oxyphilum*), Emory's sedge (*Carex emoryi*), troublesome sedge (*Carex molesta*), greater straw sedge (*Carex normalis*), pretty sedge (*Carex woodii*), common spikerush (*Eleocharis palustris*), butternut (*Juglans cinerea*), wild bergamot (*Monarda fistulosa* ssp. *brevis*), large-seed forget-me-not (*Myosotis macrosperma*), Alleghany plum (*Prunus alleghaniensis* var. *alleghaniensis*), smooth rock skullcap (*Scutellaria saxatilis*), Virginia meadowsweet (*Spiraea virginiana*), arborvitae (*Thuja occidentalis*), and downy arrowwood (*Viburnum rafinesquianum*). During the 2003–2006 floristic surveys, all but three of these species (*Agrimonia microcarpa, Carex molesta,* and *Prunus alleghaniensis* var. *alleghaniensis*) were observed in the study area. In addition, Norris documented heart-leaved skullcap (*Scutellaria ovata*), which was considered rare, threatened, or endangered at the species level at the time of his surveys. During the 2003–2006 surveys, specimens of *Scutellaria ovata* were collected and identified to the subspecific level. All our specimens were *Scutellaria ovata* ssp. *rugosa,* which is not on the current rare, threatened, or endangered plant list (WVNHP 2007). Element Occurrence Records for the 15 rare, threatened, and endangered species surveyed by Norris were entered in Biotics prior to the current project.

Rentch et al. (2005) identified 112 taxa of vascular plants during their study of vegetation patterns of the Bluestone Gorge. Two species, pretty sedge (*Carex woodii*) and matricary grapefern (*Botrychium matricariifolium*), are tracked as rare by WVNHP (2007) but neither have been entered in Biotics due to the lack of specimens and location details. *Carex woodii* was found during the 2003–2006 floristic surveys and by Norris (1992), but *Botrychium matricariifolium* was not found during either survey. Rentch et al. (2005) also listed one species, thinfruit sedge (*Carex flaccosperma*), which is not included in the Checklist and Atlas of the Vascular Flora of West Virginia (Harmon et al. 2006). According to NPSpecies (NPS 2003), *Carex flaccosperma* was collected from the study area by Bill Grafton on June 29, 1997 from the same location and on the same date as the plot record for which Grafton was listed as a surveyor (Rentch, unpublished data). The NPSpecies record of *Carex flaccosperma* is based on a nomenclatural "correction" of the Grafton collection at West Virginia University herbarium (WVU accession # 86562) which is labeled blue sedge (*Carex glaucodea*). *Carex flaccosperma* and *Carex glaucodea* are closely related taxa which have been variously treated as separate species (Ball and Reznicek 2002), as two varieties of *C. flaccosperma* (NatureServe 2007b), or as synonyms (as *C. flaccosperma* in Gleason and Cronquist 1991). The Grafton collection from BLUE identified as *Carex glaucodea* was examined by the second author, was determined to be misidentified, and was annotated as eastern woodland sedge (*Carex blanda*), a common species. Two additional specimens at West Virginia University collected by Grafton from BLUE are also labeled *Carex glaucodea*, but both of these were misidentified. One of these (WVU accession # 86533) is eastern narrowleaf sedge (*Carex amphibola*), a common species, and one (WVU accession # 60626) is limestone meadow sedge (*Carex granularis*), a species which has not been documented otherwise in the study area. Based on these annotations, *Carex flaccosperma* was not included in the annotated checklist (Appendix B) and *Carex granularis* was included.

Prior to this study, the NPSpecies database (NPS 2003) listed collections for 85 vascular plant taxa from the study area including 14 not listed in other sources and not found during the 2003–2006 field surveys. The collections identified in NPSpecies are housed in the herbaria at West Virginia University and WVNHP. In addition to the misidentification of *Carex flaccosperma* described in the previous paragraph, another error was found in the NPSpecies records. This was a Grafton collection (WVU accession # 79868) originally labeled and listed in NPSpecies as brittle bladderfern (*Cystopteris fragilis*) which was annotated correctly by Ron Fortney in 2002 as lowland bladderfern (*Cystopteris protrusa*). Based on this annotation, *Cystopteris fragilis* was not included in the annotated checklist (Appendix B).

Prior to this study, 18 occurrences of 18 vascular plant taxa tracked as rare, threatened, or endangered as of May 31, 2007 (WVNHP 2007) had been entered into Biotics.

Floristic Inventory

Six hundred sixty-eight plant taxa were identified in the park during the 2003–2006 field surveys, of which 367 were new records for the study area. Nine hundred ninety-five specimens representing 560 different vascular plant taxa were collected in the park. Eighteen taxa collected for this project are Mercer County records and 31 are Summers County records. One hundred eight taxa identified in plots during the concurrent vegetation classification and mapping project were not collected, including 47 potential county records, 30 from Mercer County and 17 from Summers County. An analysis of the state distribution (Harmon et al 2006) for the county records shows that all taxa are found in some surrounding counties. Therefore, all county records are relatively minor range extensions. Two taxa, quill sedge (*Carex tenera*) and rusty blackhaw (*Viburnum rufidulum*), collected during the 2003–2006 inventory are possible state records. Both are included in the Flora of West Virginia (Strausbaugh and Core 1977) but are not listed in the checklist by Harmon et al. (2006). According to Harmon (pers. comm., 2007), the voucher specimen identified as *Viburnum rufidulum* collected by Hutton and Bartley from Greenbrier County (WVU accession # 63259), which was referenced in Straughsbaugh and Core (1977), was annotated by Linda Rader in 1979 as withe-rod (*Viburnum nudum* var. *cassinoides*). Status of the specimens of *Carex tenera* cited by Straughsbaugh and Core (1977) has not been determined.

During the course of the 2003–2006 field surveys, an additional 51 collections were made from the vicinity outside the proclamation boundaries of the park (Figure 2). These include 12 taxa that were also documented, but not collected, in the park, and seven taxa which have not been documented inside the park but which have a high probability of occurring within the park. These nineteen taxa are listed in Table 1 along with three taxa from NPSpecies (NPS 2003) that were collected from the vicinity prior to the 2003–2006 study which have imprecise collection location data and may or may not have been collected from inside the park. These three taxa were not collected or documented in the park during the 2003–2006 surveys or from other sources.

Rare, Threatened, and Endangered Species

A total of 48 occurrences of 39 rare, threatened, and endangered vascular plants (WVNHP 2007) are currently documented from BLUE including 24 new occurrences of 18 taxa found during the 2003–2006 inventory. A list of the tracked plants found in the park including state and global conservation status ranks, federal status, and number of Element Occurrences Records in Biotics (WVDNR 2007) is provided in Table 2. Element Occurrence Records for all rare, threatened, and endangered plants known from BLUE are maintained by WVNHP in the Biotics database (WVDNR 2007).

Nine globally rare plant taxa (G1–G3, T1–T3) are known from BLUE: nightcaps (*Anemone quinquefolia* var. *minima*), American barberry (*Berberis canadensis*), Blue Ridge bittercress (*Cardamine flagellifera* var. *flagellifera*), false Indian plaintain (*Hasteola suaveolens*), wild bergamot (*Monarda fistulosa* ssp. *brevis*), smooth rock skullcap (*Scutellaria saxatilis*), Virginia meadowsweet (*Spiraea virginiana*), buffalo clover (*Trifolium reflexum*), and sand grape (*Vitis rupestris*). *Spiraea virginiana,* a federally listed threatened species, was observed once during this survey at a previously known site (Norris 1992). The site is monitored annually by the WVNHP (Harmon et al. 2007). No federally listed endangered plant species were found during the survey.

Floristic Summary

A list of 786 vascular plant taxa representing 762 species was compiled during the literature review and field work for this report (Appendix B). The 24 taxa above the number of species represent multiple subspecies or varieties per species, or identifications made to multiple taxonomic ranks. For example, cypress panicgrass (*Dichanthelium dichotomum*) is listed at the species level based on the study by Rentch et al. (2005), and three varieties of this species are listed based on our collections from the 2003–2006 surveys. In the same way, some taxa were identified at the species level in vegetation plots, but were collected elsewhere and identified to subspecies or variety. One hundred sixteen families are represented in five divisions including 102 families in the Magnoliophyta (flowering plants), eight families in the Polypodiophyta (ferns), three families in the Pinophyta (conifers), two families in the Lycopodiophyta (club mosses, spike mosses), and one family in the Equisetophyta (horsetails). The plant families with the largest representation are Asteraceae (103 taxa), Poaceae (52 taxa), Cyperaceae (52 taxa), Rosaceae (36 taxa), Fabaceae (32 taxa), Lamiaceae (33 taxa), Liliaceae (24 taxa), and Ranunculaceae (22 taxa). The largest genera represented are *Carex* (46 taxa), *Solidago* (16 taxa), *Viola* (15 taxa), *Polygonum* (12 taxa), *Symphyotrichum* (10 taxa), *Dichanthelium* (9 taxa), *Cardamine* (10 taxa), *Desmodium* (9 taxa), and *Quercus* (9 taxa).

Table 1. Plant taxa collected in the vicinity outside the boundary (with precise location data) and in the vicinity of the boundary (with imprecise location data) of Bluestone National Scenic River.

Taxa collected in 2003–2006 in the vicinity outside the park that were documented, but not collected, within the park by other sources
yellow buckeye (*Aesculus flava* Ait.)
common serviceberry*Amelanchier arborea* [Michx. f.] Fern. var. *arborea*)
sweet vernal grass (*Anthoxanthum odoratum* L. ssp. *odoratum*)
spotted knapweed (*Centaurea biebersteinii* DC.)
wild basil (*Clinopodium vulgare* L.)
pearl millet (*Pennisetum glaucum* [L.] R. Br.)
narrowleaf plantain (*Plantago lanceolata* L.)
peach (*Prunus persica* [L.] Batsch)
narrowleaf mountainmint (*Pycnanthemum tenuifolium* Schrad.)
northern red oak (*Quercus rubra* L.)
common dandelion (*Taraxacum officinale* G.H. Weber ex Wiggers ssp. *officinale*)
rue anemone (*Thalictrum thalictroides* [L.] Eames & Boivin)
Taxa collected in 2003–2006 in the vicinity outside the park that were not documented within the park by other sources
yellow fumewort (*Corydalis flavula* [Raf.] DC.)
panic grass (*Dichanthelium acuminatum* Gould & C.A. Clark ssp. *fasciculatum* [Torr.] Freckmann & Lelong)
rose of Sharon (*Hibiscus syriacus* L.)
common duckweed (*Lemna minor* L.)
Italian ryegrass (*Lolium perenne* L. ssp. *multiflorum* [Lam.] Husnot)
Britton's phlox (*Phlox subulata* L. ssp. *brittonii* [Small] Wherry)
blackeyed Susan (*Rudbeckia hirta* L. var. *pulcherrima* Farw.)
Taxa collected prior to the 2003–2006 surveys in the vicinity of the park boundary with imprecise location data that were not documented or collected in the park by the 2003–2006 surveys or other sources
reflexed sedge (*Carex retroflexa* Muhl. ex Willd.)
littleflower alumroot (*Heuchera parviflora* Bartl.)
blindeyes (*Papaver dubium* L.)

Table 2. Element Occurrence Records (EORs) of rare, threatened, and endangered plant species in Bluestone National Scenic River entered in the Biotics database as of May 31, 2007

Scientific Name	Common Name	State Rank*	Global Rank*	Federal Status*	# of EORs
Agrimonia microcarpa	smallfruit agrimony	S1	G5		1
Allium oxyphilum	Lillydale onion	S2	G2Q		3
Anemone canadensis	Canadian anemone	S1	G5		1
Anemone quinquefolia var. *minima*	nightcaps	S2	G5T3		1
Berberis canadensis	American barberry	S1	G3		3
Calycanthus floridus var. *glaucus*	eastern sweetshrub	SH	G5T5		1
Cardamine flagellifera var. *flagellifera*	Blue Ridge bittercress	S2	G3		1
Carex aggregata	glomerate sedge	S2	G5		1
Carex cumberlandensis	Cumberland sedge	S2	GNR		3
Carex emoryi	Emory's sedge	S2	G5		1
Carex hirtifolia	pubescent sedge	S2	G5		1
Carex molesta	troublesome sedge	S3	G4		1
Carex normalis	greater straw sedge	S3	G5		1
Carex tenera	quill sedge	S1	G5		1
Carex typhina	cattail sedge	S2	G5		1
Carex woodii	pretty sedge	S2	G4		1
Eleocharis palustris	common spikerush	S3	G5		1
Goodyera repens	lesser rattlesnake plantain	S1S2	G5		1
Hasteola suaveolens	false Indian plaintain	S3	G3		1
Helianthus laevigatus	smooth sunflower	S2	G4		1
Juglans cinerea	butternut	S3	G3G4		1
Juncus dichotomus	forked rush	S1	G5		1
Lemna valdiviana	valdivia duckweed	S3	G5		1
Lonicera canadensis	American fly honeysuckle	S2	G5		1
Lysimachia tonsa	southern yellow loosestrife	SH	G4		1
Monarda fistulosa ssp. *brevis*	wild bergamot	S1	G5T1		2
Myosotis macrosperma	largeseed forget-me-not	S2	G5		1
Prunus alleghaniensis var. *alleghaniensis*	Allegheny plum	S3	G4T4		1
Ribes lacustre	prickly currant	S2	G5		1
Scutellaria saxatilis	smooth rock skullcap	S2	G3		2
Spiraea virginiana	Virginia meadowsweet	S1	G2	LT	1
Stachys nuttallii	heartleaf hedgenettle	S3	G5?		1
Stachys tenuifolia	smooth hedgenettle	S3	G5		2
Taxus canadensis	Canada yew	S2S3	G5		1
Thuja occidentalis	arborvitae	S2	G5		1
Trifolium reflexum	buffalo clover	S1	G3G4		1
Viburnum rafinesquianum	downy arrowwood	S2	G5		1
Viburnum rufidulum	rusty blackhaw	S1	G5		1
Vitis rupestris	sand grape	S2	G3		1

*See Appendix A for State Rank, Global Rank, and Federal Status definitions.

16

Nativity is a representation of a species' likelihood of occurrence in West Virginia prior to European settlement. Nativity was ascertained from the Checklist and Atlas of the Vascular Flora of West Virginia (Harmon et al. 2006). A list of nativity categories and their definitions are provided in Appendix C. The flora of BLUE includes 678 native taxa, seven introduced taxa, 99 exotic taxa, one adventive taxon, and one species with unknown origin. The species of unknown origin, climbing false buckwheat (*Polygonum scandens*), has three varieties known from West Virginia (var. *cristatum*, var. *scandens*, and var. *dumetorum*); the former two are listed as native and the later as exotic. *Polygonum scandens* was identified at the species level by Oxley (1975) and in vegetation plots sampled during 2003–2006, where no specimens were collected. The herbarium at Concord University was searched for the Oxley collection of *P. scandens*, but it was not found. *Polygonum scandens* var. *cristatum* was collected four times during the 2003–2006 study, and it is likely that the records determined at the species level also represent this native taxon.

Invasive plants are species which tend to encroach into natural ecosystems in which they are not native and represent a threat to native plants in these habitats. Seventy-seven species found at BLUE are considered to be invasive in West Virginia (Harmon et al. 2006) with 28 listed as severe threats, 36 listed as significant threats, six listed as lesser threats, and seven on a watch list. Invasive ranks are defined in Appendix D.

Abundance rank is a representation of the estimated frequency of occurrence for each vascular plant in the study area. The flora of BLUE includes 30 abundant taxa, 270 common taxa, 360 uncommon taxa, and 24 rare taxa. One hundred and two taxa documented from databases and previous studies were not rediscovered during the 2003–2006 surveys and their abundances were therefore listed as unknown. Abundance ranks are defined in Appendix E and are based on the definitions used by NPSpecies (Wotawa 2004).

One objective of this project was to meet the NPS (1999) goal to "document through existing, verifiable data and targeted field investigations the occurrence of at least 90 percent of the species of vascular plants." Based on the field research and literature and database review a total of 786 plant taxa have been reported from the park, but only 621 are documented by known collections. Currently, only 79% of the taxa in the Bluestone flora checklist (Appendix B) have been vouchered with collections.

This floristic inventory covered the geography and ecological diversity of the park extremely well, in large part because it was coupled with vegetation mapping for the park. A total of 93 taxa were identified in vegetation plots during 2003–2006 but are not represented by known collections. Twelve tree species and one vine species were never collected due to height inaccessibility. A photograph of one tree species which was not collected, butternut (*Juglans cinerea*), taken in the gorge of Indian Branch, can serve as a voucher for presence of this distinctive tree in the park (Figure 3). Additional taxa were never collected because they were observed only in vegetative condition, lacking flowers or fruits which are usually considered essential diagnostic elements of quality herbarium specimens. In retrospect, vegetative collections might have been better than none. Identification of some taxa without collections may be uncertain. For example, fox sedge (*Carex vulpinoidea*), which was identified but not collected, is closely related to and easily mistaken with yellowfruit sedge (*Carex annectens*) which was collected three times. Other determinations without collections, such as the common trees yellow buckeye (*Aesculus flava*) and northern red oak (*Quercus rubra*), are highly reliable. Locations of plots with taxa that were not collected could be revisited to make collections and to reassess the correct determinations for these taxa. A database with complete plot data, including information on plot locations and species composition, was submitted as a product of vegetation mapping for the park (Vanderhorst et al. 2008).

Sixteen taxa from vegetation plots or other studies identified at the species level were collected elsewhere and identified to variety or subspecies. These species appear in the checklist at multiple taxonomic ranks and may contribute to an "over count" of the taxa which actually occur in the park.

Fifty-two of the taxa reported from BLUE but lacking known collections are based solely on Oxley's (1975) survey of Indian Branch. The Oxley report indicates that 19 of these were identified in the field but not collected. The herbarium at Concord University was searched for the remaining 33 taxa but collections were not found. However, numerous other Oxley collections from Indian Branch were found and these collections have been listed in the annotated checklist (Appendix B) for this project. The herbarium at Concord University is currently in the process of being accessioned and digitally catalogued (Tonya McKinley, pers. comm.), and it is possible that additional Oxley collections will be found that were mis-filed. Concord University is located in Athens, WV, close to BLUE, and the herbarium may house additional collections from the park. The Oxley (1975) report includes maps which show the locations where plant collections or observations were made. Locations of taxa that were observed but not collected (or the collections are lost) could be revisited to make collections and to reassess the correct determinations for these taxa.

Figure 3. Photograph of butternut (*Juglans cinerea*) taken in the gorge of Indian Branch, Bluestone National Scenic River, on April 24, 2004 (photograph by J. P. Vanderhorst).

Additional specimens from the park are also likely to be found in the herbaria of other institutions, such as Marshall University in Huntington, WV. The large number of misidentified specimens found in herbaria by the second author is an indication of human fallibility and the perils of taxonomy. Some of our collections are probably misidentified. Additional work remains to be done which could help meet the "90%" benchmark.

The flora of the park includes seven rare, threatened, or endangered plant taxa with global ranks of G1 (including T1) to G3 (including G3G4) assigned by NatureServe. For an area as small as BLUE, this is a large number of globally rare taxa, and is indicative of the regional importance of the park for conservation of plant diversity. Large population numbers of wild bergamot (*Monarda fistulosa* ssp. *brevis*) and a broad distribution of American barberry (*Berberis canadensis*) within the park are especially notable. The collection of buffalo clover (*Trifolium reflexum*) is notable because this species had not been documented in WV for over 20 years. Discovery of this species at BLUE provided rationale to change its state conservation status rank from SH to S1. It had been historically documented from nearby Barger's Springs in Summers County (Strausbaugh and Core 1977).

The small population of American fly honeysuckle (*Lonicera canadensis*) at the falls overlook on Indian Branch is currently threatened by deer herbivory and human trampling. A few shrubs of this species grow just beyond a barrier at the overlook which was in disrepair on the survey date. If repair or further development of this overlook is undertaken by NPS or WV State Parks, it may threaten these plants. However, careful development could avoid damaging these plants and could enhance the population by protecting the plants from human trampling and deer herbivory.

Deer herbivory also appears to be a threat to American barberry (*Berberis canadensis*) and is a known threat to Canada yew (*Taxus canadensis*) elsewhere in West Virginia. Although *Taxus canadensis* was not found during the 2003–2006 surveys, a large patch was reported by Oxley (1975) from Indian Branch near the upper falls. Extant populations of *Taxus canadensis* in West Virginia are usually small and visibly effected by deer herbivory. Failure to rediscover known historic populations suggests that the species may be declining in West Virginia. Monitoring populations of these three rare, palatable shrubs could provide useful information to determine optimum deer populations for a sustainable park ecosystem.

WVNHP maintains information on rare, threatened, and endangered species in its Biotics database. As new information on individual occurrences is obtained by NPS or other organizations or individuals, this information should be sent to WVNHP to add to Biotics. WVNHP will also continue to add information into Biotics based on its own surveys. The occurrence of the federally listed threatened species Virginia meadowsweet (*Spiraea virginiana*) in the park has been monitored annually by the WVNHP (Harmon et al. 2007) and these surveys will continue in the future. State and global conservation status ranks for species and Element Occurrence ranks within Biotics may change over time as new information is obtained or as population trends change. The park should consider requesting updated reports from Biotics as time passes, especially if activities are considered which may affect populations of rare, threatened, and endangered plants. The quality and utility of data in Biotics will depend on cooperation and communication between WVNHP and its partners.

Literature Cited

Bailey, R. G., P. E. Avers, T. King, and W. H. McNab. 1994. Ecoregions and subregions of the United States. USDA Forest Service [map].

Ball, P. W., and A. A. Reznicek. 2002. Carex. *In* Flora of North America north of Mexico, Volume 23, Magnoliophyta: Commelinidae (in part): Cyperaceae. Ed Flora of North America Editorial Committee. Oxford University Press. New York, NY.

Braun, E. L. 1950. Deciduous forest of eastern North America. Hafner Press. New York, NY.

Cardwell, D. H., R. B. Erwin, and H. P. Woodward. 1968. Geology map of West Virginia. West Virginia Geological and Economic Survey. Map 1. Scale 1:250000.

Englund, K. J., H. H. Arnt, T. W. Henry, C. R. Meissner Jr., J. F. Windolph Jr., and R. C. Warlow. 1977. Geologic map of the New River Gorge Area, Fayette, Raleigh, and Summers Counties, West Virginia. U. S. Geological Survey Open File Report OF-77-76-A.

Englund, K. J., P. L. Johnson, and H. H. Arndt. 1982. Geology of the New River Gorge, West Virginia. *In* New River Symposium Proceedings, May 6–8, 1982, Beckley, WV. Pp 136–145.

Flora of North America Editorial Committee, eds. 1993+. Flora of North America North of Mexico. 12+ vols. Vol. 1, 1993; Vol. 2, 1993; Vol 3., 1997; Vol. 4, 2003; Vol. 5, 2005; Vol. 19, 2006; Vol. 20, 2006; Vol. 21, 2006; Vol. 22, 2000; Vol. 23, 2002; Vol. 25, 2003; Vol. 26, 2002. Ed Flora of North America Editorial Committee. Oxford University Press. New York, NY.

Fortney, R. H., S. L. Stephenson, and H. S. Adams. 1994. Reconnaissance vegetation study of the Bluestone, New, and Gauley River Gorges. National Park Service.

Freckmann, R. W., and M. G. Lelong. 2003. Dichanthelium and Panicum sections. *In* Flora of North America North of Mexico, Volume 25, Magnoliophyta: Commelinidae (in part): Poaceae, part 2. Ed Flora of North America Editorial Committee. Oxford University Press. New York, NY.

Gebaur S., T. Howard, and T. Weldy. 2002. Theo: Herbarium Label Database. New York Natural Heritage Program. Albany, NY.

Gleason, H. A., and A. Cronquist. 1991. Manual of vascular plants of northeastern United States and adjacent Canada. Second edition. The New York Botanical Garden. Bronx, NY.

Grafton, W. N. 1993. Vascular flora on the lower sections of the Gauley, Meadow, and Bluestone rivers. WVU Extension Service. National Park Service Cooperative Agreement CA 4000-2-1016.

Harmon, P. J. 2007. Checklist of Invasive Plant Species of West Virginia. West Virginia Division of Natural Resources, Wildlife Resources Section. Elkins, WV.

Harmon, P. J., D. Ford-Werntz, and W. Grafton. 2006. Checklist and atlas of the vascular flora of West Virginia. West Virginia Division of Natural Resources, Wildlife Resources Section. Elkins, WV.

Harmon, P. J., D. Mitchell, and K. O'Malley. 2007. Performance report: West Virginia endangered plant species statewide monitoring and management federal aid in sport fish and wildlife restoration project E-2-20. West Virginia Division of Natural Resources, Wildlife Resources Section. Elkins, WV.

Jones, R. L. 2005. Plant life of Kentucky: an illustrated guide to the vascular flora. The University Press of Kentucky. Lexington, KY.

Kartesz, J. T. 1994. A synonymized checklist of the vascular flora of the United States, Canada, and Greenland. 2nd edition. 2 vols. Timber Press. Portland, OR.

Krings, A. 2004. Abaxial foliar vestiture of *Desmodium* Desv. (Fabaceae) in North Carolina and vegetative recognition of the species. Vulpina 3:140–172.

McNeal, D. W. Jr., and T. D. Jacobsen. 2002. *Allium. In* Flora of North America North of Mexico. 12+ vols. Vol. 26. Ed Flora of North America Editorial Committee. Oxford University Press. New York, NY.

National Oceanic and Atmospheric Administration (NOAA). 2002. Monthly station normals of temperature, precipitation, and heating and cooling degree days 1971–2000. Climatography of the United States No. 81. National Climatic Data Center. Ashville, NC.

National Park Service (NPS). 1999. Inventory and Monitoring Program: Guidelines for biological inventories. Last accessed Jan 24, 2006. http://www.nature.nps.gov/biology/biologicalinventories/bioinv.cfm#GuidelinesForBiologicalInentories.

National Park Service (NPS). 2000. Inventory and Monitoring Program: Eastern Rivers and Mountains Network summary of the West Virginia parks' scoping workshop, July 25, 2000. Unpublished report. Kingston, RI.

National Park Service (NPS). 2003. NPSpecies - The National Park Service Biodiversity Database. Desktop version 2.1. Last accessed March 26, 2003.

NatureServe. 2002. Element Occurrence Standard. Arlington, VA. Last accessed Jan. 22, 2008. http://www.natureserve.org/prodServices/eodraft/all.pdf.

NatureServe. 2007a. Biotics 4: Overview. Last accessed Dec. 28, 2007. Web page. http://www.natureserve.org/prodServices/biotics.jsp.

NatureServe. 2007b. NatureServe Explorer: An online encyclopedia of life [web application]. Version 6.1. NatureServe. Arlington, VA. Last accessed jan. 24, 2007. http://www.natureserve.org/explorer.

Norris, S. J. 1992. Rare species survey of Bluestone Scenic River, West Virginia. West Virginia Division of Natural Resources. National Park Service Cooperative Agreement CA 4000-0-9020.

Norris, S. J. 1999. Key to *Heuchera* in West Virginia. West Virginia Division of Natural Resources, Wildlife Resources Section. Elkins, WV.

Norris, S. J. 2002. Review of Plant Species lists for the New River Gorge National River, Bluestone National Scenic River, and Gauley Recreation Area. Final Report. National Park Service. Glen Jean, WV.

Northeast Region, National Park Service (NER NPS). November 2004 (revised September 2006). Natural and social science study proposal and deliverable guidelines. Natural Resources Report NPS/NER/NRR—2004/001. National Park Service. Philadelphia, PA.

Oxley, E. 1975. Floristics and vegetation of the gorge region of Indian Branch. Unpublished report prepared for Pipestem State Park, Pipestem, West Virginia.

Rentch, J. S., R. H. Fortney, S. L. Stephenson, H. S. Adams, W. N. Grafton, R. B. Coxe, and H. H. Mills. 2005. Vegetation patterns within the lower Bluestone River Gorge in southern West Virginia. Castanea 70(3):184–203.

Rhoads, A. F., and T. A. Block. 2000. The Plants of Pennsylvania. University of Pennsylvania Press. Philadelphia, PA.

Sotomayor, L. 2004. Terrestrial and Marine Ecoregions of the United States. The Nature Conservancy Data Sources. Global Priorities Group. http://gis.tnc.org/data/MapbookWebsite/getimage.php?id=104.

Sponaugle, K. N., D. E. McKinney, L. Wright, Jr., C. E. Nelson, R. E. Pyle, and C. L. Marra. 1984. Soil survey of Mercer and Summers Counties, West Virginia. Soil Conservation Service, U.S. Department of Agriculture. Washington, DC.

Staughsbaugh, P. D., and E. L. Core. 1977. Flora of West Virginia. Second edition. Seneca Books Inc. Morgantown, WV.

The Plant Conservation Roundtable. 1986. Guidelines for Conducting Field Botanical Surveys: Environmentally Sound Plant Collecting. 6(3).

U. S. Department of Agriculture, National Resources Conservation Service (USDA NRCS). 2007. The Plants Database. National Plant Data Center, Baton Rouge, LA 70874-4490 USA. http:// plants.usda.gov. (Accessed February 16, 2007).

U. S. Fish and Wildlife Service (USFWS). 1973. The endangered species act of 1973 as amended through the 108th Congress. http://www.fws.gov/endangered/pdfs/ESAall.pdf (Accessed January 11, 2008)

Vanderhorst, J. P., B. P. Streets, J. Jeuk, and S. C. Gawler. 2008. Vegetation Classification and Mapping of Bluestone National Scenic River, West Virginia. Technical Report NPS/NER/NRTR—2008/106. National Park Service. Philadelphia, PA.

Weakley, A. S. 2006. Flora of the Carolinas, Virginia, Georgia, and surrounding areas (Working Draft). University of North Carolina. Chapel Hill, NC.

Woods, A. J., J. M. Omernik, and D. D. Brown. 2003. Level III and level IV Ecoregions of EPA Region 3. U.S. Environmental Protection Agency. Corvallis, OR. [map]. ftp://ftp.epa.gov/wed/ecoregions/reg3/reg3_eco.pdf.

Wotawa, M. 2004. NPSpecies Data Dictionary for Users: Field and value definitions. NPSpecies 2.0. National Park Service. Fort Collins, CO.

West Virginia Division of Natural Resources (WVDNR). 2007. Biotics database records of rare species and natural communities. West Virginia Natural Heritage Program. WVDNR. Elkins, WV.

West Virginia Natural Heritage Program (WVNHP). 2007. Rare, threatened and endangered plants, February 2007. Division of Natural Resources. Elkins, WV. http://wvdnr.gov/Wildlife/documents/Plants2007_2_.pdf.

Appendix A. State and global conservation rank and federal threatened and endangered status definitions.

State Ranks

State ranks are assigned by the West Virginia Natural Heritage Program and refer to the conservation status within West Virginia.

Rank	Definition
S1	Five or fewer documented occurrences, or very few remaining individuals within the state. Extremely rare and critically imperiled; or because of some factor(s) making it especially vulnerable to extirpation.
S2	Six to 20 documented occurrences, or few remaining individuals within the state. Very rare and imperiled; or because of some factor(s) making it vulnerable to extirpation.
S3	Twenty-one to 100 documented occurrences. May be somewhat vulnerable to extirpation.
S4	Common and apparently secure with more than 100 occurrences.
S5	Very common and demonstrably secure.
SH	Historical. Species which have not been relocated within the last 20 years. May be rediscovered.
SR	Reported from state, but not yet verified.
SX	Believed extirpated. Little likelihood of rediscovery.
SU	Possibly rare, but status uncertain until more data are gathered.
S?	Unranked, or, if following a number, rank uncertain (ex. S2?).

Global Ranks

Global ranks are assigned by NatureServe and refer to the conservation status across the global range of the element.

Global basic ranks

Rank	Definition
GX	Presumed Extinct (species) - Not located despite intensive searches and virtually no likelihood of rediscovery.
	Eliminated (ecological communities) - Eliminated throughout its range, with no restoration potential due to extinction of dominant or characteristic species.
GH	Possibly Extinct (species) - Missing; known from only historical occurrences but still some hope of rediscovery.
	Presumed Eliminated - (Historic, ecological communities)-Presumed eliminated throughout its range, with no or virtually no likelihood that it will be rediscovered, but with the potential for restoration, for example, American Chestnut Forest.
G1	Critically Imperiled - At very high risk of extinction due to extreme rarity (often 5 or fewer populations), very steep declines, or other factors.
G2	Imperiled - At high risk of extinction due to very restricted range, very few populations (often 20 or fewer), steep declines, or other factors.
G3	Vulnerable - At moderate risk of extinction due to a restricted range, relatively few populations (often 80 or fewer), recent and widespread declines, or other factors.
G4	Apparently Secure - Uncommon but not rare; some cause for long-term concern due to declines or other factors.
G5	Secure - Common; widespread and abundant.

Global variant ranks

Rank	Definition
G#G#	Range Rank - A numeric range rank (e.g., G2G3) is used to indicate the range of uncertainty in the status of a species or community. A G2G3 rank would indicate that there is a roughly equal chance of G2 or G3 and other ranks are much less likely. Ranges cannot skip more than one rank (e.g., GU should be used rather than G1G4).
GU	Unrankable - Currently unrankable due to lack of information or due to substantially conflicting information about status or trends. Whenever possible, the most likely rank is assigned and a question mark qualifier may be added (e.g., G2?) to express minor uncertainty, or a range rank (e.g., G2G3) may be used to delineate the limits (range) of uncertainty.
GNR	Unranked - Global rank not yet assessed.
GNA	Not Applicable - A conservation status rank is not applicable because the species is not a suitable target for conservation activities.

Global rank qualifiers

Rank	Definition
?	Inexact Numeric Rank - Denotes some uncertainty about the numeric rank (e.g. G3? - Believed most likely a G3, but some chance of either G2 or G4).
Q	Questionable taxonomy - Taxonomic distinctiveness of this entity at the current level is questionable; resolution of this uncertainty may result in change from a species to a subspecies or hybrid, or the inclusion of this taxon in another taxon, with the resulting taxon having a lower-priority conservation priority.
C	Captive or Cultivated Only - At present extant only in captivity or cultivation, or as a reintroduced population not yet established.

Global infraspecific taxon conservation status rank - Infraspecific taxa refer to subspecies, varieties and other designations below the level of the species. Infraspecific taxon status ranks (T-ranks) apply to plants and animal species only; these T-ranks do not apply to ecological communities.

Rank	Definition
T#	Infraspecific Taxon (trinomial) - The status of infraspecific taxa (subspecies or varieties) are indicated by a "T-rank" following the species' global rank. Rules for assigning T-ranks follow the same principles outlined above for global conservation status ranks. For example, the global rank of a critically imperiled subspecies of an otherwise widespread and common species would be G5T1. A T-rank cannot imply the subspecies or variety is more abundant than the species as a whole-for example, a G1T2 cannot occur. A vertebrate animal population, such as those listed as distinct population segments under the U.S. Endangered Species Act, may be considered an infraspecific taxon and assigned a T-rank; in such cases a Q is used after the T-rank to denote the taxon's informal taxonomic status. At this time, the T rank is not used for ecological communities.

Federal Threatened and Endangered Status - Federal status is determined by the U.S. Fish and Wildlife Service. These species are protected by the Endangered Species Act of 1973, as amended through the 108th Congress.

Rank	Definition
LE	Listed Endangered. A species is threatened with extinction throughout all or a significant portion of its range.
LT	Listed Threatened. A species is likely to become endangered in the foreseeable future.

Appendix B. Annotated checklist of vascular plants known from Bluestone National Scenic River, West Virginia.

Taxa are arranged alphabetically within families which are arranged alphabetically within Divisions. Divisions are arranged in phylogenetic order starting with fern allies, then ferns, then conifers, followed by the flowering plants.

Information on each taxon includes, in the following order and format:

Division
Family
> *Scientific name* with authority (common name in parenthesis): nativity status ("native," "adventive," "introduced," or "exotic" - see Appendix C for definitions); if it is invasive ("invasive") and, if it is, invasive rank ("severe threat," "significant threat," " lesser threat," or "watch list" - see Appendix D for definitions); estimated abundance ("abundant," "common," "uncommon," "rare," or "unknown abundance" - see Appendix E for definitions); if it is tracked by West Virginia Natural Heritage Program as rare, threatened, or endangered ("WVNHP tracked") and, if it is, state rank ("S1," "S1S2," "S2," "S2S3," "S3," or "SH"), global rank ("G2," "G2Q," "G3," "G3G4," "G4," "G4T4," "G5," "G5T1," "G5T3," "G5T5," or "GNR"), and federal status ("LT") if listed (see Appendix A for rank and status definitions); if there are collections (collectors' last names and collection numbers ["S.N." if no collection number is indicated on the herbarium label]); if a collection from the 2003–2006 surveys is a state or county record ("Mercer County Record," "Summers County Record," or "WV State Record") or, if the taxon documented during the 2003–2006 surveys had been collected, the collection would have been a county record ("Potential Mercer County Record" or "Potential Summers County Record"); if the species was identified in a vegetation plot during 2003–2006 ("identified in a vegetation plot during 2003–2006"); if there are literature source(s) documenting the species occurrence in the park (author and date citations, in parenthesis).

Collections by Streets, Vanderhorst, and Short are deposited in either or both of the herbaria at West Virginia University in Morgantown, WV and the National Park Service in Glen Jean, WV. Collections by Oxley, Chapman, and Harris are deposited in the herbarium at Concord University in Athens, WV. Collections by Norris are deposited in the herbarium of the West Virginia Natural Heritage Program in Elkins, WV. All other collections are deposited at West Virginia University.

Equisetophyta

Equisetaceae

Equisetum hyemale L. var. *affine* (Engelm.) A. A. Eat. (scouringrush horsetail): native; uncommon; Streets 1351, Vanderhorst 6783; identified in a vegetation plot during 2003–2006.

Lycopodiophyta

Lycopodiaceae

Huperzia lucidula (Michx.) Trevisan (shining clubmoss): native; unknown abundance; Oxley 12, Harris S.N.; (Oxley 1975).

Lycopodium digitatum Dill. ex A. Braun (fan clubmoss): native; common; Oxley 15; identified in a vegetation plot during 2003–2006.

Lycopodium tristachyum Pursh (deeproot clubmoss): native; unknown abundance; (Rentch et al. 2005).

Selaginellaceae

Selaginella apoda (L.) Spring (meadow spikemoss): native; unknown abundance; Chapman S.N., Harris S.N.; (Oxley 1975).

Polypodiophyta

Adiantaceae

Adiantum pedatum L. (northern maidenhair): native; uncommon; Streets 1384, Vanderhorst 6929, Oxley 48; identified in a vegetation plot during 2003–2006; (Oxley 1975, Rentch et al. 2005).

Cheilanthes lanosa (Michx.) D. C. Eat. (hairy lipfern): native; uncommon; Streets 583, 604, Oxley 47; identified in a vegetation plot during 2003–2006.

Pellaea atropurpurea (L.) Link (purple cliffbrake): native; uncommon; Streets 1398a, Short 52, Grafton S.N., Oxley 45; identified in a vegetation plot during 2003–2006; (Oxley 1975).

Aspleniaceae

Asplenium ×*ebenoides* R. R. Scott (pro sp.) (Scott's spleenwort): native; uncommon; Potential Summers County record; identified in a vegetation plot during 2003–2006; (Rentch et al. 2005).

Asplenium platyneuron (L.) B. S. P. (ebony spleenwort): native; common; Streets 445b, 1443; identified in a vegetation plot during 2003–2006; (Oxley 1975, Norris 1992).

Asplenium resiliens Kunze (blackstem spleenwort): native; unknown abundance; (Oxley 1975).

Asplenium rhizophyllum L. (walking fern): native; common; Streets 1316, 1329, Grafton S.N.; identified in a vegetation plot during 2003–2006; (Oxley 1975, Norris 1992).

Asplenium trichomanes L. (maidenhair spleenwort): native; unknown abundance; Oxley 44; (Oxley 1975).

Dennstaedtiaceae

Pteridium aquilinum (L.) Kuhn (western brackenfern): native; common; identified in a vegetation plot during 2003–2006.

Dryopteridaceae

Athyrium filix-femina (L.) Roth ssp. *asplenioides* (Michx.) Hultén (asplenium ladyfern): native; uncommon; Streets 1632.

Cystopteris bulbifera (L.) Bernh. (bulblet bladderfern): native; unknown abundance; Boone 637, Oxley 30; (Oxley 1975).

Cystopteris protrusa (Weatherby) Blasdell (lowland bladderfern): native; unknown abundance; Grafton S.N.

Deparia acrostichoides (Sw.) M. Kato (silver false spleenwort): native; uncommon; Oxley 40; identified in a vegetation plot during 2003–2006; (Oxley 1975).

Diplazium pycnocarpon (Spreng.) Broun (glade fern): native; uncommon; Streets 1615; (Oxley 1975).

Dryopteris goldiana (Hook. ex Goldie) Gray (Goldie's woodfern): native; uncommon; Streets 1618; (Oxley 1975)

Dryopteris intermedia (Muhl. ex Willd.) Gray (intermediate woodfern): native; common; Streets 598, Oxley 34; identified in a vegetation plot during 2003–2006.

Dryopteris marginalis (L.) Gray (marginal woodfern): native; common; Streets 499, 1320, Vanderhorst 6614; identified in a vegetation plot during 2003–2006; (Oxley 1975, Rentch et al. 2005).

Onoclea sensibilis L. (sensitive fern): native; common; Vanderhorst 6974, Oxley 31; identified in a vegetation plot during 2003–2006; (Oxley 1975, Norris 1992).

Polystichum acrostichoides (Michx.) Schott (Christmas fern): native; abundant; Streets 518; identified in a vegetation plot during 2003–2006; (Oxley 1975, Norris 1992, Rentch et al. 2005).

Woodsia obtusa (Spreng.) Torr. ssp. *obtusa* (bluntlobe cliff fern): native; uncommon; Streets 585, Vanderhorst 7002.

Ophioglossaceae

Botrychium virginianum (L.) Sw. (rattlesnake fern): native; uncommon; Streets 1629; identified in a vegetation plot during 2003–2006; (Oxley 1975).

Osmundaceae

Osmunda cinnamomea L. (cinnamon fern): native; unknown abundance; (Norris 1992).

Osmunda claytoniana L. (interrupted fern): native; uncommon; Streets 1644; identified in a vegetation plot during 2003–2006; (Rentch et al. 2005).

Osmunda regalis L. var. *spectabilis* (Willd.) Gray (royal fern): native; uncommon; Streets 527, Grafton S.N.; identified in a vegetation plot during 2003–2006.

Polypodiaceae

Polypodium appalachianum Haufler & Windham (Appalachian polypody): native; uncommon; Vanderhorst 6818; Mercer County record; identified in a vegetation plot during 2003–2006.

Polypodium virginianum L. (rock polypody): native; common; Streets 600, Vanderhorst 6613; identified in a vegetation plot during 2003–2006; (Oxley 1975).

Thelypteridaceae

Phegopteris hexagonoptera (Michx.) Fée (broad beechfern): native; uncommon; Streets 1628; identified in a vegetation plot during 2003–2006; (Rentch et al. 2005).

Thelypteris noveboracensis (L.) Nieuwl. (New York fern): native; common; Streets 1349; identified in a vegetation plot during 2003–2006; (Norris 1992).

Pinophyta

Cupressaceae

Juniperus virginiana L. var. *virginiana* (eastern redcedar): native; uncommon; Streets 603, 1622; identified in a vegetation plot during 2003–2006; (Oxley 1975, Norris 1992, Rentch et al. 2005).

Thuja occidentalis L. (arborvitae): native; rare; WVNHP tracked, S2, G5; Streets 1424, Grafton S.N.; identified in a vegetation plot during 2003–2006; (Norris 1992).

Pinaceae

Pinus pungens Lamb. (Table Mountain pine): native; unknown abundance; (Oxley 1975, Norris 1992).

Pinus rigida P. Mill. (pitch pine): native; unknown abundance; (Oxley 1975, Norris 1992, Rentch et al. 2005).

Pinus strobus L. (eastern white pine): native; abundant; Streets 470; identified in a vegetation plot during 2003–2006; (Oxley 1975, Norris 1992, Rentch et al. 2005).

Pinus virginiana P. Mill. (Virginia pine): native; common; Vanderhorst 6759, 6772; identified in a vegetation plot during 2003–2006; (Oxley 1975, Norris 1992, Rentch et al. 2005).

Tsuga canadensis (L.) Carr. (eastern hemlock): native; abundant; Vanderhorst 6760; identified in a vegetation plot during 2003–2006; (Oxley 1975, Norris 1992, Rentch et al. 2005).

Taxaceae

Taxus canadensis Marsh. (Canada yew): native; unknown abundance; WVNHP tracked, S2S3, G5; Oxley 52; (Oxley 1975).

Magnoliophyta

Aceraceae

Acer negundo L. var. *negundo* (boxelder): native; common; Streets 343, 457, 1341; identified in a vegetation plot during 2003–2006; (Oxley 1975).

Acer nigrum Michx. f. (black maple): native; common; Streets 736a, Short 23; identified in a vegetation plot during 2003–2006.

Acer pensylvanicum L. (striped maple): native; abundant; Streets 352, 1319; identified in a vegetation plot during 2003–2006; (Oxley 1975, Norris 1992, Rentch et al. 2005).

Acer rubrum L. var. *rubrum* (red maple): native; abundant; Streets 1646; identified in a vegetation plot during 2003–2006; (Oxley 1975, Norris 1992, Rentch et al. 2005).

Acer saccharum Marsh. var. *saccharum* (sugar maple): native; abundant; Streets 323; identified in a vegetation plot during 2003–2006; (Oxley 1975, Norris 1992, Rentch et al. 2005).

Acer spicatum Lam. (mountain maple): native; rare; (Oxley 1975).

Acoraceae

Acorus calamus L. (calamus): native; uncommon; Vanderhorst 6944.

Alismataceae

Alisma subcordatum Raf. (American water plantain): native; uncommon; Streets 1343, 1408.

Sagittaria latifolia Willd. (broadleaf arrowhead): native; uncommon; Vanderhorst 7150.

Anacardiaceae

Rhus aromatica Ait. var. *aromatica* (fragrant sumac): native; common; Streets 569; identified in a vegetation plot during 2003–2006.

Rhus glabra L. (smooth sumac): native; unknown abundance; (Oxley 1975).

Rhus typhina L. (staghorn sumac): native; unknown abundance; Oxley 977; (Oxley 1975).

Toxicodendron radicans (L.) Kuntze (eastern poison ivy): native; abundant; Streets 1353, 1662; Summers County record; identified in a vegetation plot during 2003–2006; (Oxley 1975).

Toxicodendron radicans (L.) Kuntze ssp. *negundo* (Greene) Gillis (eastern poison ivy): native; abundant; identified in a vegetation plot during 2003–2006.

Annonaceae

Asimina triloba (L.) Dunal (pawpaw): native; uncommon; Streets 342, 359; identified in a vegetation plot during 2003–2006; (Rentch et al. 2005).

Apiaceae

Chaerophyllum procumbens (L.) Crantz var. *procumbens* (spreading chervil): native; uncommon; Streets 381.

Cicuta maculata L. var. *maculata* (spotted water hemlock): native; uncommon; Vanderhorst 7068; identified in a vegetation plot during 2003–2006.

Conium maculatum L. (poison hemlock): exotic; invasive, lesser threat; uncommon; Streets 549.

Cryptotaenia canadensis (L.) DC. (Canadian honewort): native; common; Streets 460, 493; identified in a vegetation plot during 2003–2006.

Daucus carota L. (Queen Anne's lace): exotic; invasive, lesser threat; abundant; Streets 681; Potential Mercer County Record; identified in a vegetation plot during 2003–2006.

Ligusticum canadense (L.) Britt. (Canadian licorice-root): native; uncommon; identified in a vegetation plot during 2003–2006.

Osmorhiza claytonii (Michx.) C. B. Clarke (Clayton's sweetroot): native; common; Streets 741, Streets 1367; identified in a vegetation plot during 2003–2006.

Osmorhiza longistylis (Torr.) DC. (longstyle sweetroot): native; common; Streets 443; identified in a vegetation plot during 2003–2006.

Sanicula canadensis L. (Canadian blacksnakeroot): native; common; identified in a vegetation plot during 2003–2006.

Sanicula canadensis L. var. *canadensis* (Canadian blacksnakeroot): native; common; Streets 573, 588, 626, 644a, 744, 1426; identified in a vegetation plot during 2003–2006.

Sanicula odorata (Raf.) K. M. Pryer & L. R. Phillippe (clustered blacksnakeroot): native; common; Streets 497, Vanderhorst 7083; identified in a vegetation plot during 2003–2006.

Sanicula trifoliata Bickn. (largefruit blacksnakeroot): native; uncommon; Streets 1369, Vanderhorst 7058; Mercer County record, Summers County record; identified in a vegetation plot during 2003–2006.

Sium suave Walt. (hemlock waterparsnip): native; uncommon; Vanderhorst 7151.

Taenidia integerrima (L.) Drude (yellow pimpernel): native; uncommon; Streets 385, Peeke S.N.; identified in a vegetation plot during 2003–2006.

Thaspium barbinode (Michx.) Nutt. (hairyjoint meadowparsnip): native; common; Streets 719; identified in a vegetation plot during 2003–2006.

Zizia aptera (Gray) Fern. (meadow zizia): native; uncommon; (Rentch et al. 2005).

Zizia aurea (L.) W. D. J. Koch (golden zizia): native; common; Streets 496, Vanderhorst 7077; identified in a vegetation plot during 2003–2006; (Rentch et al. 2005).

Zizia trifoliata (Michx.) Fern. (meadow alexanders): native; common; Streets 324, 363, Short 53; identified in a vegetation plot during 2003–2006.

Apocynaceae

Apocynum cannabinum L. (Indianhemp): native; uncommon; Streets 1358; identified in a vegetation plot during 2003–2006.

Aquifoliaceae

Ilex opaca Ait. var. *opaca* (American holly): native; unknown abundance; (Oxley 1975).

Ilex verticillata (L.) Gray (common winterberry): native; uncommon; Vanderhorst 7096, Short 35; (Norris 1992).

Araceae

Arisaema dracontium (L.) Schott (green dragon): native; uncommon; Streets 407, 454; Potential Mercer County Record; identified in a vegetation plot during 2003–2006.

Arisaema triphyllum (L.) Schott ssp. *triphyllum* (Jack in the pulpit): native; uncommon; Streets 390, Vanderhorst 6823, 7055; identified in a vegetation plot during 2003–2006; (Oxley 1975, Norris 1992, Rentch et al. 2005).

Araliaceae

Aralia nudicaulis L. (wild sarsaparilla): native; uncommon; identified in a vegetation plot during 2003–2006.

Aralia racemosa L. ssp. *racemosa* (American spikenard): native; common; Streets 1425, 1432, Boone 502; identified in a vegetation plot during 2003–2006.

Aralia spinosa L. (devil's walkingstick): native; uncommon; (Norris 1992).

Panax quinquefolius L. (American ginseng): native; uncommon; Streets 1441, Grafton S.N.; Mercer County record; identified in a vegetation plot during 2003–2006.

Aristolochiaceae

Aristolochia macrophylla Lam. (pipevine): native; uncommon; identified in a vegetation plot during 2003–2006; (Oxley 1975, Norris 1992).

Aristolochia serpentaria L. (Virginia snakeroot): native; uncommon; Streets 1571; identified in a vegetation plot during 2003–2006.

Asarum canadense L. (Canadian wildginger): native; uncommon; Streets 351; identified in a vegetation plot during 2003–2006.

Hexastylis virginica (L.) Small (Virginia heartleaf): native; uncommon; identified in a vegetation plot during 2003–2006; (Oxley 1975, Norris 1992).

Asclepiadaceae

Asclepias incarnata L. ssp. *pulchra* (Ehrh. ex Willd.) Woods. (swamp milkweed): native; uncommon; Streets 709, 1377; (Oxley 1975).

Asclepias quadrifolia Jacq. (fourleaf milkweed): native; uncommon; Streets 450; identified in a vegetation plot during 2003–2006; (Oxley 1975).

Asclepias syriaca L. (common milkweed): native; common; Streets 1406; Summers County record; identified in a vegetation plot during 2003–2006; (Oxley 1975).

Asclepias tuberosa L. (butterfly milkweed): native; unknown abundance; (Oxley 1975).

Asclepias tuberosa L. ssp. *tuberosa* (butterfly milkweed): native; uncommon; Streets 1394.

Asclepias verticillata L. (whorled milkweed): native; uncommon; Short 42; identified in a vegetation plot during 2003–2006.

Asteraceae

Achillea millefolium L. (common yarrow): exotic; common; Streets 533a, 553; identified in a vegetation plot during 2003–2006; (Oxley 1975).

Ageratina altissima (L.) King & H. E. Robins. var. *altissima* (white snakeroot): native; common; Streets 691, 1402; identified in a vegetation plot during 2003–2006; (Oxley 1975, Norris 1992, Rentch et al. 2005).

Ambrosia artemisiifolia L. var. *elatior* (L.) Descourtils (annual ragweed): native; common; Streets 713, 1419; identified in a vegetation plot during 2003–2006; (Oxley 1975).

Ambrosia trifida L. var. *trifida* (great ragweed): native; uncommon; Streets 689; Potential Mercer County Record; identified in a vegetation plot during 2003–2006; (Oxley 1975).

Anaphalis margaritacea (L.) Benth. (western pearly everlasting): native; unknown abundance; Oxley 1462; (Oxley 1975).

Antennaria plantaginifolia (L.) Richards. (woman's tobacco): native; uncommon; Streets 475, 1293b, Vanderhorst 6820; identified in a vegetation plot during 2003–2006; (Oxley 1975).

Antennaria solitaria Rydb. (singlehead pussytoes): native; uncommon; Streets 325.

Antennaria virginica Stebbins (shale barren pussytoes): native; uncommon; identified in a vegetation plot during 2003–2006.

Arnoglossum atriplicifolium (L.) H. E. Robins. (pale Indian plaintain): native; uncommon; Vanderhorst 6973, 6784; identified in a vegetation plot during 2003–2006.

Arnoglossum muehlenbergii (Schultz-Bip.) H. E. Robins. (great Indian plaintain): native; uncommon; Potential Mercer County Record, Potential Summers County record; identified in a vegetation plot during 2003–2006.

Artemisia vulgaris L. var. *vulgaris* (common wormwood): exotic; invasive, significant threat; uncommon; Streets 1575; Summers County record; identified in a vegetation plot during 2003–2006.

Bidens bipinnata L. (Spanish needles): native; uncommon; Short 45; identified in a vegetation plot during 2003–2006; (Oxley 1975).

Bidens cernua L. (nodding beggartick): native; common; Vanderhorst 6790, 7075; identified in a vegetation plot during 2003–2006.

Bidens frondosa L. (devil's beggartick): native; uncommon; Vanderhorst 7060; identified in a vegetation plot during 2003–2006; (Oxley 1975).

Bidens tripartita L. (threelobe beggarticks): native; uncommon; Short 36; identified in a vegetation plot during 2003–2006.

Bidens vulgata Greene (big devils beggartick): native; uncommon; Potential Mercer County Record; identified in a vegetation plot during 2003–2006.

Brickellia eupatorioides (L.) Shinners var. *eupatorioides* (false boneset): native; uncommon; Vanderhorst 6780.

Centaurea biebersteinii DC. (spotted knapweed): exotic; invasive, severe threat; common; (Oxley 1975).

Chrysopsis mariana (L.) Ell. (Maryland goldenaster): native; unknown abundance; (Oxley 1975).

Cichorium intybus L. (chicory): exotic; invasive, lesser threat; unknown abundance; (Oxley 1975).

Cirsium altissimum (L.) Hill (tall thistle): native; unknown abundance; (Oxley 1975).

Cirsium discolor (Muhl. ex Willd.) Spreng. (field thistle): native; uncommon; Streets 733; identified in a vegetation plot during 2003–2006.

Coreopsis auriculata L. (lobed tickseed): native; uncommon; Streets 492, Vanderhorst 6911; identified in a vegetation plot during 2003–2006; (Norris 1992).

Coreopsis major Walt. (greater tickseed): native; common; Streets 601; identified in a vegetation plot during 2003–2006; (Oxley 1975).

Coreopsis pubescens Ell. (star tickseed): native; uncommon; identified in a vegetation plot during 2003–2006.

Coreopsis tinctoria Nutt. var. *tinctoria* (golden tickseed): introduced; uncommon; Streets 650b; Potential Mercer County Record; identified in a vegetation plot during 2003–2006.

Crepis capillaris (L.) Wallr. (smooth hawksbeard): exotic; common; Streets 559.

Elephantopus carolinianus Raeusch. (Carolina elephantsfoot): native; common; Vanderhorst 7094, Grafton S.N.; identified in a vegetation plot during 2003–2006.

Erechtites hieraciifolia (L.) Raf. ex DC. var. *hieraciifolia* (American burnweed): native; common; Vanderhorst 6761, Short 13; Potential Mercer County Record; identified in a vegetation plot during 2003–2006.

Erigeron annuus (L.) Pers. (eastern daisy fleabane): native; common; Streets 524, 536, Vanderhorst 7074; identified in a vegetation plot during 2003–2006.

Erigeron philadelphicus L. var. *philadelphicus* (Philadelphia fleabane): native; uncommon; Streets 409, 441; identified in a vegetation plot during 2003–2006.

Erigeron pulchellus Michx. (robin's plantain): native; uncommon; Grafton S.N.; identified in a vegetation plot during 2003–2006; (Oxley 1975).

Erigeron strigosus Muhl. ex Willd. var. *strigosus* (prairie fleabane): native; common; Streets 602; identified in a vegetation plot during 2003–2006.

Eupatorium fistulosum Barratt (trumpetweed): native; common; Vanderhorst 7003, Short 12, 31; identified in a vegetation plot during 2003–2006; (Oxley 1975, Norris 1992).

Eupatorium perfoliatum L. var. *perfoliatum* (common boneset): native; common; Vanderhorst 6980, 7092; identified in a vegetation plot during 2003–2006; (Oxley 1975).

Eupatorium purpureum L. var. *purpureum* (sweetscented joepyeweed): native; common; identified in a vegetation plot during 2003–2006.

Eurybia divaricata (L.) Nesom (white wood aster): native; abundant; Streets 720; identified in a vegetation plot during 2003–2006; (Oxley 1975, Rentch et al. 2005).

Eurybia macrophylla (L.) Cass. (bigleaf aster): native; uncommon; Short 63; identified in a vegetation plot during 2003–2006.

Eurybia schreberi (Nees) Nees (Schreber's aster): native; uncommon; Short 24; identified in a vegetation plot during 2003–2006.

Euthamia graminifolia (L.) Nutt. var. *graminifolia* (flat-top goldentop): native; uncommon; Streets 1379.

Galinsoga quadriradiata Cav. (shaggy soldier): exotic; invasive, watch list; common; Streets 653a, 726; identified in a vegetation plot during 2003–2006.

Hasteola suaveolens (L.) Pojark. (false Indian plaintain): native; unknown abundance; WVNHP tracked, S3, G3; (Oxley 1975).

Helenium autumnale L. var. *autumnale* (common sneezeweed): native; uncommon; Streets 724, Vanderhorst 6781; identified in a vegetation plot during 2003–2006; (Oxley 1975).

Helianthus divaricatus L. (woodland sunflower): native; common; Streets 676; identified in a vegetation plot during 2003–2006; (Oxley 1975).

Helianthus laevigatus Torr. & Gray (smooth sunflower): native; unknown abundance; WVNHP tracked, S2, G4; (Oxley 1975).

Helianthus strumosus L. (paleleaf woodland sunflower): native; uncommon; Vanderhorst 7064; Mercer County record; identified in a vegetation plot during 2003–2006.

Heliopsis helianthoides (L.) Sweet var. *helianthoides* (smooth oxeye): native; uncommon; Streets 622, 638, 758; identified in a vegetation plot during 2003–2006.

Heliopsis helianthoides (L.) Sweet var. *scabra* (Dunal) Fern. (smooth oxeye): native; uncommon; Streets 682, Vanderhorst 6971, 6983; Summers County record; identified in a vegetation plot during 2003–2006.

Hieracium ×*floribundum* Wimmer & Grab. (pro sp.) (hawkweed): exotic; invasive, significant threat; unknown abundance; (Oxley 1975).

Hieracium caespitosum Dumort. (meadow hawkweed): exotic; invasive, significant threat; common; Streets 417.

Hieracium gronovii L. (queendevil): native; unknown abundance; Oxley 1567; (Oxley 1975).

Hieracium paniculatum L. (Allegheny hawkweed): native; uncommon; Potential Summers County record; identified in a vegetation plot during 2003–2006.

Hieracium venosum L. (rattlesnakeweed): native; uncommon; Streets 435, Oxley 1566; identified in a vegetation plot during 2003–2006; (Oxley 1975, Rentch et al. 2005).

Hypochaeris radicata L. (hairy catsear): exotic; uncommon; Streets 554.

Lactuca canadensis L. (Canada lettuce): native; common; Streets 1431; identified in a vegetation plot during 2003–2006.

Lactuca floridana (L.) Gaertn. (woodland lettuce): native; unknown abundance; (Oxley 1975).

Leucanthemum vulgare Lam. (oxeye daisy): exotic; invasive, significant threat; common; Streets 526; identified in a vegetation plot during 2003–2006.

Matricaria discoidea DC. (disc mayweed): introduced; uncommon; Streets 1295; Summers County record.

Packera anonyma (Wood) W. A. Weber & A. Löve (Small's ragwort): native; unknown abundance; Unknown collector S.N.

Packera aurea (L.) A. & D. Löve (golden ragwort): native; common; Streets 360; identified in a vegetation plot during 2003–2006; (Oxley 1975, Norris 1992, Rentch et al. 2005).

Packera obovata (Muhl. ex Willd.) W. A. Weber & A. Löve (roundleaf ragwort): native; uncommon; Streets 364, 472, 489; identified in a vegetation plot during 2003–2006.

Prenanthes alba L. (white rattlesnakeroot): native; uncommon; Oxley 1561; identified in a vegetation plot during 2003–2006; (Oxley 1975, Rentch et al. 2005).

Prenanthes altissima L. (tall rattlesnakeroot): native; common; Vanderhorst 6764, 7051; identified in a vegetation plot during 2003–2006.

Prenanthes serpentaria Pursh (cankerweed): native; unknown abundance; (Oxley 1975, Rentch et al. 2005).

Rudbeckia hirta L. (blackeyed Susan): native; unknown abundance; (Oxley 1975).

Rudbeckia laciniata L. var. *laciniata* (cutleaf coneflower): native; common; Streets 1573, Vanderhorst 6987; Potential Mercer County Record; identified in a vegetation plot during 2003–2006; (Oxley 1975).

Silphium trifoliatum L. var. *trifoliatum* (whorled rosinweed): native; uncommon; Streets 1348, Vanderhorst 6985; identified in a vegetation plot during 2003–2006.

Smallanthus uvedalius (L.) Mackenzie ex Small (hairy leafcup): native; common; Streets 673; identified in a vegetation plot during 2003–2006.

Solidago altissima L. (late goldenrod): native; unknown abundance; (Oxley 1975).

Solidago arguta Ait. (Atlantic goldenrod): native; unknown abundance; (Rentch et al. 2005).

Solidago arguta Ait. var. *caroliniana* Gray (Atlantic goldenrod): native; uncommon; Streets 1417, Vanderhorst 6765, 6775, 6854a, Short 51; identified in a vegetation plot during 2003–2006.

Solidago bicolor L. (white goldenrod): native; uncommon; Streets 1421, 1438, Vanderhorst 6755, Short 49; identified in a vegetation plot during 2003–2006; (Oxley 1975).

Solidago caesia L. (wreath goldenrod): native; common; Streets 1444; Mercer County record; identified in a vegetation plot during 2003–2006; (Oxley 1975, Rentch et al. 2005).

Solidago canadensis L. (Canada goldenrod): native; uncommon; Potential Mercer County Record; identified in a vegetation plot during 2003–2006.

Solidago curtisii Torr. & Gray (mountain decumbent goldenrod): native; uncommon; Streets 1446, Vanderhorst 6768, 6853, 7080; identified in a vegetation plot during 2003–2006.

Solidago flexicaulis L. (zigzag goldenrod): native; common; identified in a vegetation plot during 2003–2006.

Solidago gigantea Ait. (giant goldenrod): native; uncommon; Streets 654, 712, Vanderhorst 6998, 7069 Short 28; identified in a vegetation plot during 2003–2006; (Oxley 1975).

Solidago hispida Muhl. ex Willd. var. *hispida* (hairy goldenrod): native; common; Streets 6777b; identified in a vegetation plot during 2003–2006.

Solidago juncea Ait. var. *juncea* (early goldenrod): native; uncommon; identified in a vegetation plot during 2003–2006.

Solidago nemoralis Ait. var. *nemoralis* (gray goldenrod): native; unknown abundance; (Oxley 1975).

Solidago rugosa P. Mill. (wrinkleleaf goldenrod): native; common; Vanderhorst 7072; identified in a vegetation plot during 2003–2006.

Solidago rugosa P. Mill. ssp. *rugosa* var. *rugosa* (wrinkleleaf goldenrod): native; common; Short 60; Summers County record; identified in a vegetation plot during 2003–2006.

Solidago sphacelata Raf. (autumn goldenrod): native; uncommon; Streets 696, Streets 1390, 1391, Short 50, Grafton S.N.; identified in a vegetation plot during 2003–2006.

Solidago ulmifolia Muhl. ex Willd. var. *ulmifolia* (elmleaf goldenrod): native; uncommon; Streets 700, Vanderhorst 6758, 6777a, 6779, 6972; identified in a vegetation plot during 2003–2006; (Oxley 1975).

Sonchus asper (L.) Hill ssp. *asper* (spiny sowthistle): exotic; invasive, significant threat; common; Streets 1357; identified in a vegetation plot during 2003–2006.

Symphyotrichum cordifolium (L.) Nesom (common blue wood aster): native; uncommon; Vanderhorst 6766, 7056; identified in a vegetation plot during 2003–2006; (Rentch et al. 2005).

Symphyotrichum dumosum (L.) Nesom (rice button aster): native; unknown abundance; (Oxley 1975).

Symphyotrichum laeve (L.) A. & D. Löve var. *laeve* (smooth blue aster): native; uncommon; Short 46, 66; identified in a vegetation plot during 2003–2006.

Symphyotrichum lateriflorum (L.) A. & D. Löve (calico aster): native; uncommon; Vanderhorst 6785, 7082; identified in a vegetation plot during 2003–2006.

Symphyotrichum patens (Ait.) Nesom var. *patens* (late purple aster): native; uncommon; Vanderhorst 6763; identified in a vegetation plot during 2003–2006.

Symphyotrichum pilosum (Willd.) Nesom var. *pilosum* (hairy white oldfield aster): native; uncommon; Vanderhorst 6786, 6793.

Symphyotrichum praealtum (Poir.) Nesom (willowleaf aster): native; uncommon; Potential Summers County record; identified in a vegetation plot during 2003–2006.

Symphyotrichum prenanthoides (Muhl. ex Willd.) Nesom (crookedstem aster): native; common; Vanderhorst 6795, 7067, 7081; identified in a vegetation plot during 2003–2006; (Oxley 1975).

Symphyotrichum puniceum (L.) A. & D. Löve var. *puniceum* (purplestem aster): native; uncommon; identified in a vegetation plot during 2003–2006.

Symphyotrichum undulatum (L.) Nesom (wavyleaf aster): native; uncommon; Vanderhorst 6757; identified in a vegetation plot during 2003–2006.

Taraxacum officinale G. H. Weber ex Wiggers ssp. *officinale* (common dandelion): exotic; abundant; identified in a vegetation plot during 2003–2006; (Oxley 1975).

Tussilago farfara L. (coltsfoot): exotic; invasive, significant threat; abundant; Streets 322; identified in a vegetation plot during 2003–2006; (Oxley 1975).

Verbesina alternifolia (L.) Britt. ex Kearney (wingstem): native; common; Streets 703, Vanderhorst 7065; identified in a vegetation plot during 2003–2006; (Rentch et al. 2005).

Verbesina occidentalis (L.) Walt. (yellow crownbeard): native; uncommon; Vanderhorst 6788, 7088; identified in a vegetation plot during 2003–2006.

Vernonia gigantea (Walt.) Trel. ssp. *gigantea* (giant ironweed): native; uncommon; Streets 715, Vanderhorst 7046, 7078, Short 32; identified in a vegetation plot during 2003–2006.

Vernonia noveboracensis (L.) Michx. (New York ironweed): native; uncommon; Oxley 1359; identified in a vegetation plot during 2003–2006; (Oxley 1975).

Xanthium strumarium L. (rough cockleburr): native; uncommon; identified in a vegetation plot during 2003–2006.

Xanthium strumarium L. var. *glabratum* (DC.) Cronq. (rough cockleburr): native; uncommon; Vanderhorst 6789.

Balsaminaceae

Impatiens capensis Meerb. (jewelweed): native; uncommon; Vanderhorst 6992, 7071, Short 38; identified in a vegetation plot during 2003–2006; (Oxley 1975).

Impatiens pallida Nutt. (pale touch-me-not): native; uncommon; Vanderhorst 7085; (Oxley 1975).

Berberidaceae

Berberis canadensis P. Mill. (American barberry): native; rare; WVNHP tracked, S1, G3; Streets 1275, 1648, Vanderhorst 6752; identified in a vegetation plot during 2003–2006; (Oxley 1975).

Berberis vulgaris L. (common barberry): exotic; common; identified in a vegetation plot during 2003–2006.

Caulophyllum giganteum (Farw.) Loconte & Blackwell (giant blue cohosh): native; common; Streets 335.

Caulophyllum thalictroides (L.) Michx. (blue cohosh): native; common; Potential Summers County record; identified in a vegetation plot during 2003–2006; (Oxley 1975, Norris 1992, Rentch et al. 2005).

Podophyllum peltatum L. (mayapple): native; common; Streets 1651, Peeke S.N.; identified in a vegetation plot during 2003–2006; (Oxley 1975, Norris 1992).

Betulaceae

Alnus serrulata (Ait.) Willd. (hazel alder): native; uncommon; Streets 671, Vanderhorst 6938, 7070; identified in a vegetation plot during 2003–2006; (Oxley 1975, Norris 1992).

Betula alleghaniensis Britt. var. *alleghaniensis* (yellow birch): native; unknown abundance; (Oxley 1975).

Betula lenta L. (sweet birch): native; uncommon; Vanderhorst 6615; identified in a vegetation plot during 2003–2006; (Oxley 1975, Rentch et al. 2005).

Betula nigra L. (river birch): native; common; Streets 1645, Vanderhorst 6942; identified in a vegetation plot during 2003–2006; (Oxley 1975, Norris 1992).

Carpinus caroliniana Walt. ssp. *Virginiana* (Marsh.) Furlow (American hornbeam): native; common; Streets 456; identified in a vegetation plot during 2003–2006; (Oxley 1975, Norris 1992, Rentch et al. 2005).

Corylus americana Walt. (American hazelnut): native; uncommon; Streets 1584, Vanderhorst 7048; identified in a vegetation plot during 2003–2006; (Oxley 1975).

Ostrya virginiana (P. Mill.) K. Koch var. *virginiana* (hophornbeam): native; common; identified in a vegetation plot during 2003–2006; (Oxley 1975, Rentch et al. 2005).

Bignoniaceae

Campsis radicans (L.) Seem. ex Bureau (trumpet creeper): native; uncommon; Streets 1403.

Catalpa bignonioides Walt. (southern catalpa): introduced; invasive, watch list; uncommon; identified in a vegetation plot during 2003–2006.

Catalpa speciosa (Warder) Warder ex Engelm. (northern catalpa): introduced; uncommon; identified in a vegetation plot during 2003–2006.

Boraginaceae

Cynoglossum virginianum L. var. *virginianum* (wild comfrey): native; common; Streets 449; identified in a vegetation plot during 2003–2006.

Hackelia virginiana (L.) I. M. Johnston (beggarslice): native; common; Short 48, Grafton S.N.; identified in a vegetation plot during 2003–2006.

Lithospermum latifolium Michx. (American stoneseed): native; uncommon; Streets 453, Grafton S.N.; identified in a vegetation plot during 2003–2006.

Myosotis macrosperma Engelm. (largeseed forget-me-not): native; uncommon; WVNHP tracked, S2, G5; Streets 433, Grafton S.N.; identified in a vegetation plot during 2003–2006; (Norris 1992).

Myosotis verna Nutt. (spring forget-me-not): native; uncommon; Streets 383; identified in a vegetation plot during 2003–2006.

Brassicaceae

Alliaria petiolata (Bieb.) Cavara & Grande (garlic mustard): exotic; invasive, severe threat; common; Streets 355; identified in a vegetation plot during 2003–2006; (Oxley 1975).

Arabis laevigata (Muhl. ex Willd.) Poir. var. *laevigata* (smooth rockcress): native; uncommon; Streets 442, Peeke S.N.; (Oxley 1975).

Barbarea verna (P. Mill.) Aschers. (early yellowrocket): exotic; unknown abundance; Tosh 34S; (Oxley 1975).

Barbarea vulgaris Ait. f. (garden yellowrocket): exotic; common; Streets 367; Potential Summers County record; identified in a vegetation plot during 2003–2006; (Oxley 1975)Brassica napus L. (rape): exotic; unknown abundance; (Oxley 1975).

Brassica nigra (L.) W. D. J. Koch (black mustard): exotic; common; Streets 652a, 1345, 1356; identified in a vegetation plot during 2003–2006.

Brassica rapa L. var. *rapa* (field mustard): exotic; invasive, watch list; unknown abundance; (Oxley 1975).

Cardamine angustata O. E. Schulz (slender toothwort): native; uncommon; Vanderhorst 6828; identified in a vegetation plot during 2003–2006; (Oxley 1975).

Cardamine bulbosa (Schreb. ex Muhl.) B. S. P. (bulbous bittercress): native; uncommon; Streets 366; identified in a vegetation plot during 2003–2006; (Oxley 1975, Norris 1992).

Cardamine concatenata (Michx.) Sw. (cutleaf toothwort): native; common; Streets 318; identified in a vegetation plot during 2003–2006; (Oxley 1975).

Cardamine diphylla (Michx.) Wood (crinkleroot): native; common; Streets 356; (Oxley 1975).

Cardamine flagellifera O. E. Schulz var. *flagellifera* (Blue Ridge bittercress): native; unknown abundance; WVNHP tracked, S2, G3; Grafton S.N.

Cardamine hirsuta L. (hairy bittercress): native; uncommon; Vanderhorst 6762; identified in a vegetation plot during 2003–2006.

Cardamine impatiens L. (narrowleaf bittercress): exotic; uncommon; Streets 429, Grafton S.N.; identified in a vegetation plot during 2003–2006.

Cardamine parviflora L. var. *arenicola* (Britt.) O. E. Schulz (sand bittercress): native; uncommon; Potential Summers County record; identified in a vegetation plot during 2003–2006.

Cardamine pensylvanica Muhl. ex Willd. (Pennsylvania bittercress): native; uncommon; Streets 403; identified in a vegetation plot during 2003–2006; (Oxley 1975).

Cardamine rotundifolia Michx. (American bittercress): native; uncommon; Streets 1290; Summers County record.

Draba ramosissima Desv. (branched draba): native; uncommon; Streets 584; identified in a vegetation plot during 2003–2006; (Oxley 1975).

Erucastrum gallicum (Willd.) O. E. Schulz (common dogmustard): exotic; unknown abundance; (Oxley 1975).

Hesperis matronalis L. (dames rocket): exotic; invasive, severe threat; common; Streets 431, 1347; identified in a vegetation plot during 2003–2006; (Norris 1992).

Lepidium campestre (L.) Ait. f. (field pepperweed): exotic; invasive, significant threat; common; Streets 382.

Lepidium virginicum L. (Virginia pepperweed): native; unknown abundance; Boone S.N.

Raphanus raphanistrum L. (wild radish): exotic; invasive, significant threat; uncommon; Streets 1412.

Rorippa nasturtium-aquaticum (L.) Hayek (watercress): introduced; invasive, significant threat; unknown abundance; (Oxley 1975).

Rorippa sylvestris (L.) Bess. (creeping yellowcress): exotic; invasive, severe threat; uncommon; Streets 525, 639, 1344, Grafton S.N.; Mercer County record; identified in a vegetation plot during 2003–2006.

Calycanthaceae

Calycanthus floridus L. var. *glaucus* (Willd.) Torr. & Gray (eastern sweetshrub): native; unknown abundance; WVNHP tracked, SH, G5T5; Boone S.N.

Campanulaceae

Campanula divaricata Michx. (small bonny bellflower): native; uncommon; Streets 1399, Vanderhorst 6927; identified in a vegetation plot during 2003–2006; (Oxley 1975).

Campanulastrum americanum (L.) Small (American bellflower): native; common; Streets 680; identified in a vegetation plot during 2003–2006.

Lobelia cardinalis L. (cardinalflower): native; uncommon; Vanderhorst 6966, 6986; identified in a vegetation plot during 2003–2006; (Oxley 1975).

Lobelia inflata L. (Indian-tobacco): native; common; Streets 642, 651b, Vanderhorst 7059; identified in a vegetation plot during 2003–2006; (Oxley 1975).

Lobelia siphilitica L. var. *siphilitica* (great blue lobelia): native; uncommon; Streets 1436, Vanderhorst 6782, Short 26; identified in a vegetation plot during 2003–2006; (Oxley 1975).

Triodanis perfoliata (L.) Nieuwl. (clasping Venus' looking-glass): native; common; Streets 545.

Cannabaceae

Humulus japonicus Sieb. & Zucc. (Japanese hop): exotic; invasive, lesser threat; common; Streets 1430, 1652, Grafton S.N.; identified in a vegetation plot during 2003–2006.

Caprifoliaceae

Lonicera canadensis Bartr. ex Marsh. (American fly honeysuckle): native; rare; WVNHP tracked, S2, G5; Vanderhorst 6817; (Oxley 1975).

Lonicera dioica L. (limber honeysuckle): native; unknown abundance; (Oxley 1975).

Lonicera japonica Thunb. (Japanese honeysuckle): exotic; invasive, severe threat; common; Streets 532; identified in a vegetation plot during 2003–2006; (Oxley 1975).

Lonicera morrowii Gray (Morrow's honeysuckle): exotic; invasive, severe threat; common; Streets 405.

Sambucus nigra L. ssp. *canadensis* (L.) R. Bolli (common elderberry): native; common; Streets 551; identified in a vegetation plot during 2003–2006; (Oxley 1975).

Sambucus racemosa L. var. *racemosa* (red elderberry): native; unknown abundance; Oxley 1342; (Oxley 1975).

Viburnum acerifolium L. (mapleleaf viburnum): native; abundant; Streets 1333a; identified in a vegetation plot during 2003–2006; (Oxley 1975).

Viburnum dentatum L. var. *dentatum* (southern arrowwood): native; uncommon; Streets 1667, Vanderhorst 6925; Summers County record; identified in a vegetation plot during 2003–2006; (Oxley 1975).

Viburnum prunifolium L. (blackhaw): native; common; identified in a vegetation plot during 2003–2006; (Oxley 1975, Norris 1992).

Viburnum rafinesquianum J. A. Schultes (downy arrowwood): native; common; WVNHP tracked, S2, G5; Streets 572, 1282, Vanderhorst 6558, 7061, Grafton S.N.; identified in a vegetation plot during 2003–2006; (Norris 1992).

Viburnum rufidulum Raf. (rusty blackhaw): native; uncommon; WVNHP tracked, S1, G5; Streets 386, 1630; WV State record.

Caryophyllaceae

Cerastium arvense L. ssp. *strictum* (L.) Ugborogho (field chickweed): native; unknown abundance; (Oxley 1975).

Cerastium glomeratum Thuill. (sticky chickweed): exotic; invasive, significant threat; common; Streets 1287; identified in a vegetation plot during 2003–2006.

Dianthus armeria L. (Deptford pink): exotic; invasive, watch list; uncommon; Streets 552; (Oxley 1975).

Myosoton aquaticum (L.) Moench (giantchickweed): exotic; invasive, significant threat; uncommon; Streets 594, 1297; identified in a vegetation plot during 2003–2006.

Paronychia canadensis (L.) Wood (smooth forked nailwort): native; uncommon; Streets 695, Vanderhorst 6756, Short 55; identified in a vegetation plot during 2003–2006; (Rentch et al. 2005).

Paronychia fastigiata (Raf.) Fern. var. *paleacea* Fern. (hairy forked nailwort): native; uncommon; Streets 570, 590; Potential Mercer County Record; identified in a vegetation plot during 2003–2006.

Saponaria officinalis L. (bouncingbet): exotic; invasive, significant threat; common; Streets 683, Streets 1352; identified in a vegetation plot during 2003–2006.

Silene caroliniana Walt. ssp. *pensylvanica* (Michx.) Clausen (Pennsylvania catchfly): native; uncommon; Streets 379, Oxley 634; identified in a vegetation plot during 2003–2006; (Oxley 1975).

Silene stellata (L.) Ait. f. (widowsfrill): native; common; Streets 698, Streets 1401, Short 1401; Potential Mercer County Record; identified in a vegetation plot during 2003–2006.

Silene virginica L. (fire pink): native; unknown abundance; Oxley 634b; (Oxley 1975).

Silene vulgaris (Moench) Garcke (maidenstears): exotic; unknown abundance; Oxley 632; (Oxley 1975).

Stellaria graminea L. (grasslike starwort): exotic; invasive, significant threat; uncommon; Streets 424, 463.

Stellaria longifolia Muhl. ex Willd. var. *longifolia* (longleaf starwort): native; common; identified in a vegetation plot during 2003–2006.

Stellaria media (L.) Vill. ssp. *media* (common chickweed): exotic; invasive, severe threat; common; Streets 1633; identified in a vegetation plot during 2003–2006.

Stellaria media (L.) Vill. ssp. *pallida* (Dumort.) Aschers. & Graebn. (common chickweed): exotic; invasive, severe threat; common; Streets 337, 389; Summers County record; identified in a vegetation plot during 2003–2006.

Stellaria pubera Michx. (star chickweed): native; common; Streets 345b; identified in a vegetation plot during 2003–2006; (Oxley 1975, Norris 1992, Rentch et al. 2005).

Celastraceae

Celastrus scandens L. (American bittersweet): native; unknown abundance; (Oxley 1975).

Euonymus americana L. (bursting-heart): native; uncommon; Potential Summers County record; identified in a vegetation plot during 2003–2006.

Euonymus atropurpurea Jacq. var. *atropurpurea* (eastern wahoo): native; rare; identified in a vegetation plot during 2003–2006.

Chenopodiaceae

Chenopodium ambrosioides L. var. *ambrosioides* (Mexican tea): exotic; invasive, lesser threat; common; Streets 1569; identified in a vegetation plot during 2003–2006.

Clusiaceae

Hypericum ellipticum Hook. (pale St. Johnswort): native; uncommon; Potential Mercer County Record; identified in a vegetation plot during 2003–2006.

Hypericum mutilum L. (dwarf St. Johnswort): native; uncommon; Streets 655; identified in a vegetation plot during 2003–2006.

Hypericum perforatum L. (common St. Johnswort): exotic; invasive, watch list; uncommon; identified in a vegetation plot during 2003–2006; (Rentch et al. 2005).

Hypericum prolificum L. (shrubby St. Johnswort): native; uncommon; Streets 729, Boone 269; identified in a vegetation plot during 2003–2006.

Hypericum punctatum Lam. (spotted St. Johnswort): native; uncommon; Streets 645a, 651a, 1386, 1574; identified in a vegetation plot during 2003–2006.

Commelinaceae

Commelina communis L. var. *communis* (Asiatic dayflower): exotic; uncommon; Streets 686, Short 18; identified in a vegetation plot during 2003–2006.

Tradescantia ohiensis Raf. (bluejacket): native; uncommon; Streets 530, 596, Grafton S.N.; identified in a vegetation plot during 2003–2006.

Tradescantia virginiana L. (Virginia spiderwort): native; uncommon; Potential Mercer County Record; identified in a vegetation plot during 2003–2006.

Convolvulaceae

Ipomoea pandurata (L.) G. F. W. Mey. (man of the earth): native; uncommon; Streets 621, 678, 1359, Vanderhorst 6996; identified in a vegetation plot during 2003–2006.

Cornaceae

Cornus amomum P. Mill. (silky dogwood): native; common; Streets 1374, Short 61; identified in a vegetation plot during 2003–2006; (Norris 1992).

Cornus florida L. (flowering dogwood): native; common; Streets 353, 377; identified in a vegetation plot during 2003–2006; (Norris 1992, Rentch et al. 2005).

Cornus racemosa Lam. (gray dogwood): native; uncommon; identified in a vegetation plot during 2003–2006.

Nyssa sylvatica Marsh. (blackgum): native; common; identified in a vegetation plot during 2003–2006; (Rentch et al. 2005).

Crassulaceae

Sedum ternatum Michx. (woodland stonecrop): native; abundant; Streets 370, 394; identified in a vegetation plot during 2003–2006; (Oxley 1975, Norris 1992).

Cucurbitaceae

Sicyos angulatus L. (oneseed burr cucumber): native; uncommon; Streets 723, 1337, Vanderhorst 6943; identified in a vegetation plot during 2003–2006.

Cyperaceae

Carex aggregata Mackenzie (glomerate sedge): native; uncommon; WVNHP tracked, S2, G5; Vanderhorst 6566, 6572.

Carex albursina Sheldon (white bear sedge): native; uncommon; Streets 546; identified in a vegetation plot during 2003–2006; (Rentch et al. 2005).

Carex amphibola Steud. (eastern narrowleaf sedge): native; common; Streets 410a, 427, 762, 766, 1312b, Vanderhorst 6563, Grafton S.N.; identified in a vegetation plot during 2003–2006.

Carex annectens (Bickn.) Bickn. (yellowfruit sedge): native; uncommon; Streets 411, 560, 644b; identified in a vegetation plot during 2003–2006.

Carex blanda Dewey (eastern woodland sedge): native; uncommon; Streets 410b, 479, 482, Vanderhorst 6562, 6611, Grafton S.N.; identified in a vegetation plot during 2003–2006.

Carex bromoides Schkuhr ex Willd. ssp. *bromoides* (bromelike sedge): native; rare; Vanderhorst 6915; Summers County record.

Carex caroliniana Schwein. (Carolina sedge): native; uncommon; Streets 412, 541b, Vanderhorst 6914, 6921, 6941; identified in a vegetation plot during 2003–2006.

Carex cephalophora Muhl. ex Willd. (oval–leaf sedge): native; uncommon; Streets 491; identified in a vegetation plot during 2003–2006.

Carex communis Bailey var. *communis* (fibrousroot sedge): native; uncommon; Streets 375, 397, Vanderhorst 6824, 6829; Mercer County record, Summers County record; identified in a vegetation plot during 2003–2006.

Carex conjuncta Boott (soft fox sedge): native; unknown abundance; Grafton S.N.

Carex crinita Lam. var. *crinita* (fringed sedge): native; uncommon; Streets 430, 1340, Vanderhorst 6920; identified in a vegetation plot during 2003–2006.

Carex cumberlandensis Naczi, Kral & Bryson (Cumberland sedge): native; uncommon; WVNHP tracked, S2, GNR; Streets 756, 1312a, Vanderhorst 6610, 6902; Potential Mercer County Record; identified in a vegetation plot during 2003–2006.

Carex digitalis Willd. var. *digitalis* (slender woodland sedge): native; common; Streets 500, 759, Vanderhorst 6604, Grafton S.N.; identified in a vegetation plot during 2003–2006.

Carex emoryi Dewey (Emory's sedge): native; common; WVNHP tracked, S2, G5; Vanderhorst 6913; identified in a vegetation plot during 2003–2006; (Norris 1992).

Carex frankii Kunth (Frank's sedge): native; uncommon; Streets 567, 731, Vanderhorst 7044, 7047; identified in a vegetation plot during 2003–2006.

Carex gracilescens Steud. (slender looseflower sedge): native; uncommon; Vanderhorst 6567.

Carex gracillima Schwein. (graceful sedge): native; uncommon; Streets 738, 1293a, Vanderhorst 6571, 6577, 6922; identified in a vegetation plot during 2003–2006.

Carex granularis Muhl. ex Willd. (limestone meadow sedge): native; unknown abundance; Grafton S.N.

Carex hirsutella Mackenzie (fuzzy wuzzy sedge): native; uncommon; Streets 483, 517, 541a, 754, 1311, 1413, Vanderhorst 6606, Grafton S.N.; identified in a vegetation plot during 2003–2006; (Rentch et al. 2005).

Carex hirtifolia Mackenzie (pubescent sedge): native; rare; WVNHP tracked, S2, G5; Vanderhorst 6575.

Carex hitchcockiana Dewey (Hitchcock's sedge): native; uncommon; Streets 742, 761, Vanderhorst 6564; identified in a vegetation plot during 2003–2006.

Carex jamesii Schwein. (James' sedge): native; uncommon; Streets 515, Vanderhorst 6567, Grafton S.N.; identified in a vegetation plot during 2003–2006.

Carex laxiculmis Schwein. var. *laxiculmis* (spreading sedge): native; uncommon; Streets 1364; identified in a vegetation plot during 2003–2006.

Carex laxiflora Lam. (broad looseflower sedge): native; uncommon; Streets 395a, 481, 511, 539, 765; identified in a vegetation plot during 2003–2006; (Rentch et al. 2005).

Carex lupulina Muhl. ex Willd. (hop sedge): native; uncommon; Streets 1435, Vanderhorst 6939, 6976; Summers County record; identified in a vegetation plot during 2003–2006.

Carex lurida Wahlenb. (shallow sedge): native; common; Streets 1339, Vanderhorst 6569; identified in a vegetation plot during 2003–2006.

Carex molesta Mackenzie ex Bright (troublesome sedge): native; unknown abundance; WVNHP tracked, S3, G4; Phillips S.N.; (Norris 1992).

Carex normalis Mackenzie (greater straw sedge): native; uncommon; WVNHP tracked, S3, G5; Streets 466, Grafton S.N.; (Norris 1992).

Carex oligocarpa Schkuhr ex Willd. (richwoods sedge): native; uncommon; Streets 760; identified in a vegetation plot during 2003–2006.

Carex pensylvanica Lam. (Pennsylvania sedge): native; common; Streets 473, 514, Vanderhorst 6832; identified in a vegetation plot during 2003–2006; (Rentch et al. 2005).

Carex plantaginea Lam. (plantainleaf sedge): native; uncommon; Vanderhorst 6831; Potential Summers County record; identified in a vegetation plot during 2003–2006; (Rentch et al. 2005).

Carex platyphylla Carey (broadleaf sedge): native; uncommon; Streets 395b, Vanderhorst 6830; identified in a vegetation plot during 2003–2006.

Carex prasina Wahlenb. (drooping sedge): native; uncommon; Streets 509; identified in a vegetation plot during 2003–2006.

Carex radiata (Wahlenb.) Small (eastern star sedge): native; uncommon; Streets 421,490, 575, 763, 764, Vanderhorst 6559, 6565, 6609; identified in a vegetation plot during 2003–2006.

Carex rosea Schkuhr ex Willd. (rosy sedge): native; unknown abundance; Grafton S.N.

Carex sparganioides Muhl. ex Willd. (burr reed sedge): native; uncommon; Streets 571.

Carex squarrosa L. (squarrose sedge): native; uncommon; Vanderhorst 6917, 6937, Grafton S.N.; identified in a vegetation plot during 2003–2006; (Rentch et al. 2005).

Carex stipata Muhl. ex Willd. var. *stipata* (owlfruit sedge): native; uncommon; Streets 418, 556, Vanderhorst 6916; identified in a vegetation plot during 2003–2006.

Carex swanii (Fern.) Mackenzie (Swan's sedge): native; common; Streets 498; identified in a vegetation plot during 2003–2006.

Carex tenera Dewey (quill sedge): native; rare; WVNHP tracked, S1, G5; Vanderhorst 6570; WV State record.

Carex torta Boott ex Tuckerman (twisted sedge): native; common; Vanderhorst 6573.

Carex tribuloides Wahlenb. var. *tribuloides* (blunt broom sedge): native; uncommon; Streets 561, Streets 1354; identified in a vegetation plot during 2003–2006.

Carex typhina Michx. (cattail sedge): native; rare; WVNHP tracked, S2, G5; Streets 413b.

Carex vulpinoidea Michx. (fox sedge): native; uncommon; identified in a vegetation plot during 2003–2006.

Carex willdenowii Schkuhr ex Willd. (Willdenow's sedge): native; uncommon; Streets 576, Vanderhorst 6607, 6612; identified in a vegetation plot during 2003–2006.

Carex woodii Dewey (pretty sedge): native; rare; WVNHP tracked, S2, G4; Vanderhorst 6854b; identified in a vegetation plot during 2003–2006; (Norris 1992, Rentch et al. 2005).

Cyperus strigosus L. (strawcolored flatsedge): native; common; Streets 711, 647b, Vanderhorst 6975, 6800, 7045; identified in a vegetation plot during 2003–2006.

Eleocharis palustris (L.) Roemer & J. A. Schultes (common spikerush): native; rare; WVNHP tracked, S3, G5; Norris S.N.

Eleocharis tenuis (Willd.) J. A. Schultes var. *tenuis* (slender spikerush): native; common; Vanderhorst 6919; Summers County record; identified in a vegetation plot during 2003–2006.

Scirpus cyperinus (L.) Kunth (woolgrass): native; common; Streets 1380, 1381, Vanderhorst 7089; identified in a vegetation plot during 2003–2006.

Scirpus pendulus Muhl. (rufous bulrush): native; unknown abundance; Grafton S.N.

Scirpus polyphyllus Vahl (leafy bulrush): native; common; Streets 562, Vanderhorst 7090; Mercer County record; identified in a vegetation plot during 2003–2006.

Diapensiaceae

Galax urceolata (Poir.) Brummitt (beetleweed): native; unknown abundance; Grafton S.N.; (Oxley 1975).

Dioscoreaceae

Dioscorea oppositifolia L. (Chinese yam): exotic; invasive, severe threat; unknown abundance; Grafton S.N.

Dioscorea quaternata J. F. Gmel. (fourleaf yam): native; abundant; Streets 1621; Summers County record; identified in a vegetation plot during 2003–2006; (Oxley 1975, Norris 1992, Rentch et al. 2005).

Dioscorea villosa L. (wild yam): native; unknown abundance; (Rentch et al. 2005).

Dipsacaceae

Dipsacus fullonum L. (Fuller's teasel): exotic; invasive, significant threat; uncommon; Streets 666, 714; identified in a vegetation plot during 2003–2006.

Ebenaceae

Diospyros virginiana L. (common persimmon): native; uncommon; identified in a vegetation plot during 2003–2006.

Elaeagnaceae

Elaeagnus umbellata Thunb. var. *parvifolia* (Royle) Schneid. (autumn olive): exotic; invasive, severe threat; common; Streets 380; Summers County record; identified in a vegetation plot during 2003–2006.

Ericaceae

Epigaea repens L. (trailing arbutus): native; uncommon; Oxley 1124; identified in a vegetation plot during 2003–2006; (Oxley 1975).

Gaultheria procumbens L. (eastern teaberry): native; uncommon; Vanderhorst 7062; identified in a vegetation plot during 2003–2006; (Oxley 1975, Rentch et al. 2005).

Gaylussacia baccata (Wangenh.) K. Koch (black huckleberry): native; uncommon; Vanderhorst 6909; Potential Mercer County Record; identified in a vegetation plot during 2003–2006.

Kalmia latifolia L. (mountain laurel): native; uncommon; Streets 488; identified in a vegetation plot during 2003–2006; (Oxley 1975).

Oxydendrum arboreum (L.) DC. (sourwood): native; abundant; identified in a vegetation plot during 2003–2006; (Oxley 1975, Norris 1992, Rentch et al. 2005).

Rhododendron arborescens (Pursh) Torr. (smooth azalea): native; uncommon; Streets 1583; identified in a vegetation plot during 2003–2006.

Rhododendron calendulaceum (Michx.) Torr. (flame azalea): native; uncommon; Streets 401; (Oxley 1975).

Rhododendron maximum L. (great laurel): native; common; Streets 597, 401; identified in a vegetation plot during 2003–2006; (Oxley 1975, Norris 1992).

Rhododendron periclymenoides (Michx.) Shinners (pink azalea): native; unknown abundance; (Oxley 1975).

Rhododendron prinophyllum (Small) Millais (early azalea): native; unknown abundance; (Oxley 1975).

Vaccinium pallidum Ait. (Blue Ridge blueberry): native; common; Streets 1623, Oxley 1120; identified in a vegetation plot during 2003–2006; (Oxley 1975).

Vaccinium stamineum L. (deerberry): native; common; Vanderhorst 6907; identified in a vegetation plot during 2003–2006; (Oxley 1975)

Euphorbiaceae

Acalypha gracilens Gray var. *gracilens* (slender threeseed mercury): native; uncommon; Streets 1577; Summers County record; identified in a vegetation plot during 2003–2006.

Acalypha rhomboidea Raf. (common threeseed mercury): native; uncommon; Streets 1404, Vanderhorst 6981, 6988, Short 14a; identified in a vegetation plot during 2003–2006.

Acalypha virginica L. (Virginia threeseed mercury): native; uncommon; Potential Mercer County Record; identified in a vegetation plot during 2003–2006.

Euphorbia corollata L. (flowering spurge): native; uncommon; Streets 620, 675, Vanderhorst 6991; identified in a vegetation plot during 2003–2006.

Fabaceae

Albizia julibrissin Durazz. (silktree): exotic; invasive, significant threat; common; identified in a vegetation plot during 2003–2006.

Amphicarpaea bracteata (L.) Fern. (American hogpeanut): native; abundant; Streets 694, 747; identified in a vegetation plot during 2003–2006.

Apios americana Medik. (groundnut): native; uncommon; Streets 649b, Short 34; identified in a vegetation plot during 2003–2006; (Rentch et al. 2005).

Astragalus canadensis L. var. *canadensis* (Canadian milkvetch): native; uncommon; Streets 1400.

Cercis canadensis L. var. *canadensis* (eastern redbud): native; abundant; Streets 362; identified in a vegetation plot during 2003–2006; (Oxley 1975, Norris 1992, Rentch et al. 2005).

Coronilla varia L. (crownvetch): exotic; invasive, severe threat; common; Streets 531; Potential Mercer County Record; identified in a vegetation plot during 2003–2006.

Desmodium canadense (L.) DC. (showy ticktrefoil): native; unknown abundance; (Oxley 1975).

Desmodium ciliare (Muhl. ex Willd.) DC. var. *ciliare* (hairy small-leaf ticktrefoil): native; uncommon; Vanderhorst 6767, 6791.

Desmodium cuspidatum (Muhl. ex Willd.) DC. ex Loud. var. *cuspidatum* (largebract ticktrefoil): native; uncommon; Streets 674.

Desmodium glabellum (Michx.) DC. (Dillenius' ticktrefoil): native; uncommon; Vanderhorst 6984a; identified in a vegetation plot during 2003–2006; (Oxley 1975).

Desmodium glutinosum (Muhl. ex Willd.) Wood (pointedleaf ticktrefoil): native; uncommon; Streets 672, Short 27; Mercer County record; identified in a vegetation plot during 2003–2006.

Desmodium nudiflorum (L.) DC. (nakedflower ticktrefoil): native; common; Potential Summers County record; identified in a vegetation plot during 2003–2006.

Desmodium obtusum (Muhl. ex Willd.) DC. (stiff ticktrefoil): native; uncommon; Streets 688; identified in a vegetation plot during 2003–2006.

Desmodium paniculatum (L.) DC. var. *paniculatum* (panicledleaf ticktrefoil): native; uncommon; Streets 702, Vanderhorst 6984b; identified in a vegetation plot during 2003–2006.

Desmodium rotundifolium DC. (prostrate ticktrefoil): native; uncommon; Streets 751, 1392; identified in a vegetation plot during 2003–2006.

Gleditsia triacanthos L. (honeylocust): native; uncommon; Streets 1661, Grafton S.N.; identified in a vegetation plot during 2003–2006.

Lathyrus venosus Muhl. ex Willd. (veiny pea): native; uncommon; Streets 1576, 1655, Oxley 932; identified in a vegetation plot during 2003–2006.

Lespedeza cuneata (Dum.-Cours.) G. Don (sericea lespedeza): exotic; invasive, severe threat; common; Streets 1568; identified in a vegetation plot during 2003–2006.

Lespedeza frutescens (L.) Hornem. (shrubby lespedeza): native; common; Vanderhorst 6770, 6778, 6999, Short 47; identified in a vegetation plot during 2003–2006; (Oxley 1975).

Lespedeza hirta (L.) Hornem. ssp. hirta (hairy lespedeza): native; uncommon; Short 64.

Lespedeza procumbens Michx. (trailing lespedeza): native; common; Streets 699, Vanderhorst 6773; identified in a vegetation plot during 2003–2006.

Lespedeza violacea (L.) Pers. (violet lespedeza): native; common; Streets 697, Vanderhorst 6978; identified in a vegetation plot during 2003–2006.

Medicago lupulina L. (black medick): exotic; invasive, significant threat; common; Streets 1361, Short *68*; identified in a vegetation plot during 2003–2006.

Melilotus officinalis (L.) Lam. (yellow sweetclover): exotic; invasive, significant threat; common; Streets 529a, 646b; identified in a vegetation plot during 2003–2006; (Oxley 1975).

Robinia pseudoacacia L. (black locust): native; abundant; Streets 444; identified in a vegetation plot during 2003–2006; (Oxley 1975, Norris 1992, Rentch et al. 2005).

Senna hebecarpa (Fern.) Irwin & Barneby (American senna): native; uncommon; Streets 1342, 1407, Vanderhorst 7053; identified in a vegetation plot during 2003–2006.

Trifolium campestre Schreb. (field clover): exotic; invasive, significant threat; common; Streets 533b; (Oxley 1975).

Trifolium hybridum L. (alsike clover): exotic; invasive, significant threat; common; Streets 650a; identified in a vegetation plot during 2003–2006.

Trifolium pratense L. (red clover): exotic; invasive, lesser threat; common; Streets 593; identified in a vegetation plot during 2003–2006; (Oxley 1975).

Trifolium reflexum L. (buffalo clover): native; rare; WVNHP tracked, S1, G3G4; Streets 540.

Trifolium repens L. (white clover): exotic; invasive, significant threat; common; Streets 440, Vanderhorst 6912; identified in a vegetation plot during 2003–2006; (Oxley 1975).

Vicia caroliniana Walt. (Carolina vetch): native; common; Streets 374, 542, Oxley 931; identified in a vegetation plot during 2003–2006; (Oxley 1975, Rentch et al. 2005).

Fagaceae

Castanea dentata (Marsh.) Borkh. (American chestnut): native; uncommon; (Oxley 1975).

Fagus grandifolia Ehrh. (American beech): native; common; Vanderhorst 7079; identified in a vegetation plot during 2003–2006; (Oxley 1975, Norris 1992, Rentch et al. 2005).

Quercus alba L. (white oak): native; abundant; Streets 1292; identified in a vegetation plot during 2003–2006; (Oxley 1975, Norris 1992, Rentch et al. 2005).

Quercus coccinea Muenchh. var. *coccinea* (scarlet oak): native; common; Streets 1422; identified in a vegetation plot during 2003–2006; (Oxley 1975, Norris 1992, Rentch et al. 2005).

Quercus falcata Michx. (southern red oak): native; unknown abundance; Grafton S.N.

Quercus muehlenbergii Engelm. (chinkapin oak): native; common; Short 41; identified in a vegetation plot during 2003–2006; (Rentch et al. 2005).

Quercus palustris Muenchh. (pin oak): native; unknown abundance; (Oxley 1975).

Quercus prinus L. (chestnut oak): native; abundant; Streets 1656a; identified in a vegetation plot during 2003–2006; (Oxley 1975, Norris 1992, Rentch et al. 2005).

Quercus rubra L. (northern red oak): native; abundant; identified in a vegetation plot during 2003–2006; (Oxley 1975, Norris 1992, Rentch et al. 2005).

Quercus stellata Wangenh. (post oak): native; uncommon; Streets 1388; identified in a vegetation plot during 2003–2006; (Oxley 1975, Norris 1992, Rentch et al. 2005).

Quercus velutina Lam. (black oak): native; common; identified in a vegetation plot during 2003–2006; (Oxley 1975, Norris 1992, Rentch et al. 2005).

Fumariaceae

Dicentra canadensis (Goldie) Walp. (squirrel corn): native; unknown abundance; Oxley 682; (Oxley 1975).

Dicentra cucullaria (L.) Bernh. (dutchman's breeches): native; common; Streets 331; (Oxley 1975).

Gentianaceae

Gentianella quinquefolia (L.) Small ssp. *quinquefolia* (agueweed): native; unknown abundance; (Oxley 1975).

Geraniaceae

Geranium bicknellii Britt. (Bicknell's cranesbill): native; uncommon; Streets 469.

Geranium maculatum L. (spotted geranium): native; common; Streets 365, Vanderhorst 6822; identified in a vegetation plot during 2003–2006; (Oxley 1975, Norris 1992, Rentch et al. 2005).

Grossulariaceae

Ribes cynosbati L. (eastern prickly gooseberry): native; uncommon; Streets 580, Vanderhorst 6819; (Oxley 1975).

Ribes lacustre (Pers.) Poir. (prickly currant): native; unknown abundance; WVNHP tracked, S2, G5; Grafton S.N.

Hamamelidaceae

Hamamelis virginiana L. (American witchhazel): native; abundant; Streets 406, 1368; identified in a vegetation plot during 2003–2006; (Oxley 1975, Norris 1992, Rentch et al. 2005).

Hippocastanaceae

Aesculus flava Ait. (yellow buckeye): native; abundant; identified in a vegetation plot during 2003–2006; (Oxley 1975, Norris 1992, Rentch et al. 2005).

Hydrangeaceae

Hydrangea arborescens L. (wild hydrangea): native; common; Streets 1324; identified in a vegetation plot during 2003–2006; (Oxley 1975).

Hydrocharitaceae

Elodea canadensis Michx. (Canadian waterweed): native; unknown abundance; Grafton S.N.

Hydrophyllaceae

Hydrophyllum canadense L. (bluntleaf waterleaf): native; common; Vanderhorst 6934; identified in a vegetation plot during 2003–2006.

Hydrophyllum virginianum L. (eastern waterleaf): native; uncommon; Streets 1291, 1314; identified in a vegetation plot during 2003–2006; (Oxley 1975).

Iridaceae

Iris pseudacorus L. (paleyellow iris): exotic; invasive, significant threat; uncommon; Streets 462; identified in a vegetation plot during 2003–2006.

Sisyrinchium angustifolium P. Mill. (narrowleaf blue-eyed grass): native; common; Streets 413a; identified in a vegetation plot during 2003–2006.

Juglandaceae

Carya alba (L.) Nutt. ex Ell. (mockernut hickory): native; common; Streets 503, 592, 1397, 1656b; Potential Mercer County Record; identified in a vegetation plot during 2003–2006; (Oxley 1975, Rentch et al. 2005).

Carya cordiformis (Wangenh.) K. Koch (bitternut hickory): native; common; Vanderhorst 7091; identified in a vegetation plot during 2003–2006; (Oxley 1975).

Carya glabra (P. Mill.) Sweet (pignut hickory): native; common; identified in a vegetation plot during 2003–2006; (Oxley 1975, Rentch et al. 2005).

Carya ovata (P. Mill.) K. Koch (shagbark hickory): native; common; Streets 1398b; Summers County record; identified in a vegetation plot during 2003–2006; (Oxley 1975, Rentch et al. 2005).

Juglans cinerea L. (butternut): native; uncommon; WVNHP tracked, S3, G3G4; identified in a vegetation plot during 2003–2006; (Norris 1992).

Juglans nigra L. (black walnut): native; uncommon; identified in a vegetation plot during 2003–2006; (Oxley 1975, Rentch et al. 2005).

Juncaceae

Juncus dichotomus Ell. (forked rush): native; rare; WVNHP tracked, S1, G5; Streets 1585; Summers County record; identified in a vegetation plot during 2003–2006.

Juncus effusus L. (common rush): native; common; identified in a vegetation plot during 2003–2006.

Juncus effusus L. var. *solutus* Fern. & Wieg. (lamp rush): native; common; Streets 665; identified in a vegetation plot during 2003–2006.

Juncus tenuis Willd. (poverty rush): native; common; Streets 568; identified in a vegetation plot during 2003–2006.

Luzula acuminata Raf. var. *acuminata* (hairy woodrush): native; common; Vanderhorst 6904; Summers County record; identified in a vegetation plot during 2003–2006.

Luzula multiflora (Ehrh.) Lej. ssp. *multiflora* var. *multiflora* (common woodrush): native; common; Streets 484, Vanderhorst 6605; identified in a vegetation plot during 2003–2006.

Lamiaceae

Blephilia ciliata (L.) Benth. (downy pagoda-plant): native; uncommon; Streets 538.

Clinopodium vulgare L. (wild basil): native; common; (Oxley 1975).

Collinsonia canadensis L. (richweed): native; uncommon; Streets 640, Short 25; identified in a vegetation plot during 2003–2006; (Oxley 1975).

Cunila origanoides (L.) Britt. (common dittany): native; uncommon; Vanderhorst 6774, Short 44; identified in a vegetation plot during 2003–2006; (Oxley 1975, Rentch et al. 2005).

Glechoma hederacea L. (ground ivy): exotic; invasive, severe threat; common; Streets 344; identified in a vegetation plot during 2003–2006.

Lamium purpureum L. var. *purpureum* (purple deadnettle): exotic; invasive, significant threat; common; Streets 387, 1631.

Lycopus uniflorus Michx. var. *uniflorus* (northern bugleweed): native; common; Potential Summers County record; identified in a vegetation plot during 2003–2006.

Lycopus virginicus L. (Virginia water horehound): native; common; Streets 749, Short 30; Mercer County record; identified in a vegetation plot during 2003–2006.

Meehania cordata (Nutt.) Britt. (Meehan's mint): native; common; Streets 494B, Grafton S.N.; identified in a vegetation plot during 2003–2006; (Oxley 1975).

Mentha arvensis L. (wild mint): native; uncommon; Streets 645b, Short 29; Mercer County record; identified in a vegetation plot during 2003–2006.

Monarda clinopodia L. (white bergamot): native; uncommon; Streets 1318, Vanderhorst 6928; identified in a vegetation plot during 2003–2006.

Monarda fistulosa L. (wild bergamot): native; unknown abundance; (Oxley 1975, Norris 1992, Rentch et al. 2005).

Monarda fistulosa L. ssp. *brevis* (Fosberg & Artz) Scora, comb. nov. ined. (wild bergamot): native; common; WVNHP tracked, S1, G5T1; Streets 485, 587, 1372; identified in a vegetation plot during 2003–2006; (Norris 1992).

Monarda fistulosa L. ssp. *fistulosa* var. *mollis* (L.) Benth. (wild bergamot): native; rare; Streets 701, Vanderhorst 6935; Summers County record.

Perilla frutescens (L.) Britt. (beefsteakplant): exotic; invasive, severe threat; uncommon; Vanderhorst 6794, Streets 7086; Mercer County record.

Physostegia virginiana (L.) Benth. ssp. *virginiana* (obedient plant): native; uncommon; Streets 623, 1346, Grafton S.N.; identified in a vegetation plot during 2003–2006.

Prunella vulgaris L. (common selfheal): exotic; common; Streets 595; identified in a vegetation plot during 2003–2006; (Oxley 1975).

Pycnanthemum incanum (L.) Michx. var. *incanum* (hoary mountainmint): native; uncommon; identified in a vegetation plot during 2003–2006.

Pycnanthemum pycnanthemoides (Leavenworth) Fern. var. *pycnanthemoides* (southern mountainmint): native; uncommon; Streets 693.

Pycnanthemum tenuifolium Schrad. (narrowleaf mountainmint): native; uncommon; identified in a vegetation plot during 2003–2006.

Salvia lyrata L. (lyreleaf sage): native; common; Streets 432; identified in a vegetation plot during 2003–2006.

Scutellaria elliptica Muhl. Ex Spreng. var. *elliptica* (hairy skullcap): native; uncommon; Streets 516, 562, 1387b; identified in a vegetation plot during 2003–2006.

Scutellaria elliptica Muhl. ex Spreng. var. *hirsuta* (Short & Peter) Fern. (hairy skullcap): native; uncommon; Streets 1325; Summers County record.

Scutellaria lateriflora L. var. *lateriflora* (blue skullcap): native; uncommon; Streets 730; identified in a vegetation plot during 2003–2006.

Scutellaria nervosa Pursh (veiny skullcap): native; uncommon; Streets 439, 452; identified in a vegetation plot during 2003–2006; (Oxley 1975).

Scutellaria ovata Hill (heartleaf skullcap): native; uncommon; identified in a vegetation plot during 2003–2006; (Norris 1992).

Scutellaria ovata Hill ssp. *rugosa* (Wood) Epling (heartleaf skullcap): native; uncommon; Streets 494A, Streets 579; identified in a vegetation plot during 2003–2006.

Scutellaria parvula Michx. var. *missouriensis* (Torr.) Goodman & Lawson (Leonard's skullcap): native; unknown abundance; (Oxley 1975).

Scutellaria saxatilis Riddell (smooth rock skullcap): native; uncommon; WVNHP tracked, S2, G3; Streets 1387a, Vanderhorst 6616, Norris S.N.; identified in a vegetation plot during 2003–2006; (Norris 1992).

Scutellaria serrata Andr. (showy skullcap): native; unknown abundance; Oxley 1220t; (Oxley 1975).

Stachys nuttallii Shuttlw. ex Benth. (heartleaf hedgenettle): native; uncommon; WVNHP tracked, S3, G5?; Vanderhorst 6618, 7066; identified in a vegetation plot during 2003–2006.

Stachys tenuifolia Willd. (smooth hedgenettle): native; uncommon; WVNHP tracked, S3, G5; Streets 658, Streets 669; identified in a vegetation plot during 2003–2006.

Teucrium canadense L. var. *canadense* (Canada germander): native; uncommon; Vanderhorst 6931, 6936, 6982, Unkown collector S.N.; identified in a vegetation plot during 2003–2006.

Lauraceae

Lindera benzoin (L.) Blume var. *pubescens* (Palmer & Steyermark) Rehd. (northern spicebush): native; common; Vanderhorst 6930, 7063; identified in a vegetation plot during 2003–2006.

Sassafras albidum (Nutt.) Nees (sassafras): native; common; identified in a vegetation plot during 2003–2006; (Oxley 1975, Norris 1992, Rentch et al. 2005).

Lemnaceae

Lemna valdiviana Phil. (valdivia duckweed): native; rare; WVNHP tracked, S3, G5; Vanderhorst 7152.

Liliaceae

Allium canadense L. var. *canadense* (meadow garlic): native; uncommon; Streets 416b, 521, 555; identified in a vegetation plot during 2003–2006.

Allium cernuum Roth var. *cernuum* (nodding onion): native; uncommon; (Oxley 1975, Norris 1992).

Allium oxyphilum Wherry (Lillydale onion): native; rare; WVNHP tracked, S2, G2Q; Streets 1415, 1423, Short 58a; identified in a vegetation plot during 2003–2006; (Norris 1992).

Allium vineale L. ssp. *vineale* (wild garlic): exotic; invasive, significant threat; common; identified in a vegetation plot during 2003–2006.

Clintonia umbellulata (Michx.) Morong (white clintonia): native; uncommon; Streets 1570; identified in a vegetation plot during 2003–2006; (Oxley 1975).

Convallaria majalis L. (European lily of the valley): exotic; unknown abundance; Oxley 443; (Oxley 1975).

Convallaria majuscula Greene (American lily-of-the-valley): native; unknown abundance; (Norris 1992).

Erythronium americanum Ker-Gawl. ssp. americanum (dogtooth violet): native; unknown abundance; Oxley 436; (Oxley 1975).

Erythronium umbilicatum Parks & Hardin ssp. *umbilicatum* (dimpled troutlily): native; uncommon; Streets 319.

Hypoxis hirsuta (L.) Coville (common goldstar): native; uncommon; Streets 371; identified in a vegetation plot during 2003–2006.

Maianthemum canadense Desf. (Canada mayflower): native; common; Oxley 440; identified in a vegetation plot during 2003–2006; (Oxley 1975).

Maianthemum racemosum (L.) Link ssp. *racemosum* (feathery false lily of the valley): native; common; Streets 1657, 1663; identified in a vegetation plot during 2003–2006; (Oxley 1975, Norris 1992, Rentch et al. 2005).

Medeola virginiana L. (Indian cucumber): native; common; identified in a vegetation plot during 2003–2006.

Narcissus pseudonarcissus L. (daffodil): introduced; uncommon; Streets 361a.

Polygonatum biflorum (Walt.) Ell. (smooth Solomon's seal): native; common; Streets 465; identified in a vegetation plot during 2003–2006; (Oxley 1975, Rentch et al. 2005).

Polygonatum pubescens (Willd.) Pursh (hairy Solomon's seal): native; common; Streets 372, 1619; identified in a vegetation plot during 2003–2006; (Rentch et al. 2005).

Prosartes lanuginosa (Michx.) D. Don (yellow fairybells): native; common; Streets 1638, 1643, Vanderhorst 6926, 7054; identified in a vegetation plot during 2003–2006; (Oxley 1975, Rentch et al. 2005).

Trillium erectum L. (red trillium): native; common; Streets 350; identified in a vegetation plot during 2003–2006; (Oxley 1975, Norris 1992).

Trillium grandiflorum (Michx.) Salisb. (white trillium): native; common; Streets 376; (Oxley 1975).

Trillium sessile L. (toadshade): native; uncommon; Streets 332.

Trillium undulatum Willd. (painted trillium): native; uncommon; identified in a vegetation plot during 2003–2006.

Uvularia grandiflora Sm. (largeflower bellwort): native; common; Streets 368, 1637.

Uvularia perfoliata L. (perfoliate bellwort): native; common; Streets 1625, Peeke S.N.; identified in a vegetation plot during 2003–2006; (Oxley 1975).

Uvularia sessilifolia L. (sessileleaf bellwort): native; uncommon; Vanderhorst 7006; identified in a vegetation plot during 2003–2006; (Oxley 1975).

Linaceae

Linum striatum Walt. (ridged yellow flax): native; uncommon; Streets 1375.

Lythraceae

Cuphea viscosissima Jacq. (blue waxweed): native; common; Streets 677.

Lythrum salicaria L. (purple loosestrife): exotic; invasive, severe threat; uncommon; Streets 710, 1405, Vanderhorst 6967, Short 39; identified in a vegetation plot during 2003–2006.

Magnoliaceae

Liriodendron tulipifera L. (tuliptree): native; abundant; Streets 459; identified in a vegetation plot during 2003–2006; (Oxley 1975, Norris 1992, Rentch et al. 2005).

Magnolia acuminata (L.) L. (cucumber-tree): native; common; identified in a vegetation plot during 2003–2006; (Oxley 1975, Norris 1992, Rentch et al. 2005).

Magnolia tripetala (L.) L. (umbrella-tree): native; unknown abundance; Boone S.N.

Menispermaceae

Menispermum canadense L. (common moonseed): native; uncommon; identified in a vegetation plot during 2003–2006.

Molluginaceae

Mollugo verticillata L. (green carpetweed): adventive; uncommon; Streets 1410.

Monotropaceae

Monotropa hypopithys L. (pinesap): native; uncommon; Streets 505; identified in a vegetation plot during 2003–2006.

Monotropa uniflora L. (Indianpipe): native; common; Streets 507, 605; identified in a vegetation plot during 2003–2006; (Oxley 1975).

Moraceae

Morus rubra L. var. *rubra* (red mulberry): native; common; Oxley 354; identified in a vegetation plot during 2003–2006; (Oxley 1975).

Nymphaeaceae

Nuphar lutea (L.) Sm. ssp. *advena* (Ait.) Kartesz & Gandhi (yellow pond-lily): native; uncommon; Streets 1653.

Oleaceae

Chionanthus virginicus L. (white fringetree): native; uncommon; Streets 1280; identified in a vegetation plot during 2003–2006; (Oxley 1975).

Fraxinus americana L. (white ash): native; abundant; Streets 486, Boone 248; identified in a vegetation plot during 2003–2006; (Oxley 1975, Norris 1992, Rentch et al. 2005).

Fraxinus pennsylvanica Marsh. (green ash): native; common; Streets 1665; Potential Mercer County Record; identified in a vegetation plot during 2003–2006.

Ligustrum vulgare L. (European privet): exotic; invasive, significant threat; uncommon; Streets 1296; identified in a vegetation plot during 2003–2006.

Onagraceae

Circaea lutetiana L. ssp. *canadensis* (L.) Aschers. & Magnus (broadleaf enchanter's nightshade): native; common; Streets 1327; Potential Mercer County Record; identified in a vegetation plot during 2003–2006.

Epilobium coloratum Biehler (purpleleaf willowherb): native; uncommon; Vanderhorst 7087.

Oenothera fruticosa L. ssp. *fruticosa* (narrowleaf evening-primrose): native; uncommon; Streets 534, Grafton S.N.

Oenothera parviflora L. (northern evening-primrose): native; uncommon; Streets 652b; identified in a vegetation plot during 2003–2006.

Orchidaceae

Aplectrum hyemale (Muhl. ex Willd.) Torr. (Adam and Eve): native; unknown abundance; (Oxley 1975).

Cypripedium acaule Ait. (moccasin flower): native; uncommon; Vanderhorst 6910; identified in a vegetation plot during 2003–2006; (Oxley 1975).

Cypripedium parviflorum Salisb. (lesser yellow lady's slipper): native; unknown abundance; (Oxley 1975).

Cypripedium parviflorum Salisb. var. *pubescens* (Willd.) Knight (greater yellow lady's slipper): native; unknown abundance; Grafton S.N.

Galearis spectabilis (L.) Raf. (showy orchid): native; rare; Streets 1666; (Rentch et al. 2005).

Goodyera pubescens (Willd.) R. Br. ex Ait. f. (downy rattlesnake plantain): native; uncommon; Streets 618, 684, Grafton S.N.; identified in a vegetation plot during 2003–2006; (Oxley 1975, Rentch et al. 2005).

Goodyera repens (L.) R. Br. ex Ait. f. (lesser rattlesnake plantain): native; unknown abundance; WVNHP tracked, S1S2, G5; (Oxley 1975).

Isotria verticillata Raf. (large whorled pogonia): native; unknown abundance; Grafton S.N.

Liparis liliifolia (L.) L. C. Rich. ex Ker-Gawl. (brown widelip orchid): native; rare; Vanderhorst 6906; identified in a vegetation plot during 2003–2006.

Platanthera lacera (Michx.) G. Don (green fringed orchid): native; uncommon; Streets 606.

Platanthera orbiculata (Pursh) Lindl. (lesser roundleaved orchid): native; uncommon; Potential Summers County record; identified in a vegetation plot during 2003–2006.

Spiranthes cernua (L.) L. C. Rich. (nodding lady's tresses): native; unknown abundance; (Oxley 1975).

Spiranthes lacera (Raf.) Raf. (northern slender lady's tresses): native; unknown abundance; Oxley 478; (Oxley 1975).

Tipularia discolor (Pursh) Nutt. (crippled cranefly): native; uncommon; Streets 1414.

Orobanchaceae

Conopholis americana (L.) Wallr. f. (American cancer-root): native; common; Oxley 1302; identified in a vegetation plot during 2003–2006; (Oxley 1975).

Epifagus virginiana (L.) W. Bart. (beechdrops): native; uncommon; identified in a vegetation plot during 2003–2006; (Oxley 1975).

Orobanche uniflora L. (oneflowered broomrape): native; uncommon; Grafton S.N.; (Oxley 1975).

Oxalidaceae

Oxalis corniculata L. (creeping woodsorrel): exotic; uncommon; Streets 746; identified in a vegetation plot during 2003–2006.

Oxalis dillenii Jacq. (slender yellow woodsorrel): native; uncommon; Streets 414, 467; identified in a vegetation plot during 2003–2006.

Oxalis grandis Small (great yellow woodsorrel): native; common; Streets 445a; Potential Mercer County Record; identified in a vegetation plot during 2003–2006; (Norris 1992, Rentch et al. 2005).

Oxalis montana Raf. (mountain woodsorrel): native; unknown abundance; (Oxley 1975)

Oxalis stricta L. (common yellow oxalis): native; common; Streets 728, Short 16; identified in a vegetation plot during 2003–2006; (Rentch et al. 2005).

Oxalis violacea L. (violet woodsorrel): native; uncommon; Streets 392, 422, Peeke S.N.; identified in a vegetation plot during 2003–2006.

Papaveraceae

Sanguinaria canadensis L. (bloodroot): native; common; Streets 321; identified in a vegetation plot during 2003–2006; (Oxley 1975, Norris 1992, Rentch et al. 2005).

Passifloraceae

Passiflora lutea L. (yellow passionflower): native; uncommon; Potential Mercer County Record; identified in a vegetation plot during 2003–2006.

Phytolaccaceae

Phytolacca americana L. var. *americana* (American pokeweed): native; common; Oxley 607; identified in a vegetation plot during 2003–2006; (Oxley 1975).

Plantaginaceae

Plantago lanceolata L. (narrowleaf plantain): exotic; common; (Oxley 1975).

Plantago rugelii Dcne. var. *rugelii* (blackseed plantain): native; common; Streets 634, 664; identified in a vegetation plot during 2003–2006.

Plantago virginica L. (Virginia plantain): native; uncommon; Streets 1279.

Platanaceae

Platanus occidentalis L. (American sycamore): native; common; Streets 1604; Potential Mercer County Record; identified in a vegetation plot during 2003–2006; (Oxley 1975, Norris 1992, Rentch et al. 2005).

Poaceae

Agrostis capillaris L. (colonial bentgrass): exotic; invasive, significant threat; uncommon; Potential Summers County record; identified in a vegetation plot during 2003–2006.

Agrostis gigantea Roth (redtop): native; common; Streets 662, 667; identified in a vegetation plot during 2003–2006.

Agrostis perennans (Walt.) Tuckerman (upland bentgrass): native; common; Streets 692, 717; identified in a vegetation plot during 2003–2006.

Andropogon gerardii Vitman (big bluestem): native; common; Streets 647a; identified in a vegetation plot during 2003–2006.

Anthoxanthum odoratum L. ssp. *odoratum* (sweet vernalgrass): exotic; common; identified in a vegetation plot during 2003–2006.

Brachyelytrum erectum (Schreb. ex Spreng.) Beauv. (bearded shorthusk): native; uncommon; Streets 743, 1322, 1365; identified in a vegetation plot during 2003–2006; (Rentch et al. 2005).

Bromus commutatus Schrad. (bald brome): exotic; invasive, severe threat; common; Streets 565.

Bromus kalmii Gray (arctic brome): native; uncommon; Streets 577, Grafton S.N.

Bromus pubescens Muhl. ex Willd. (hairy woodland brome): native; common; Streets 513, 522, 589, 646a 718, 1332, 1418, Short 57.

Chasmanthium latifolium (Michx.) Yates (Indian woodoats): native; uncommon; Streets 624, 637; identified in a vegetation plot during 2003–2006.

Cinna arundinacea L. (sweet woodreed): native; common; Streets 636, 740, Vanderhorst 6796, 6940, 7000, Short 33; identified in a vegetation plot during 2003–2006.

Dactylis glomerata L. ssp. *glomerata* (orchardgrass): exotic; invasive, significant threat; common; Streets 415; identified in a vegetation plot during 2003–2006.

Danthonia compressa Austin ex Peck (flattened oatgrass): native; uncommon; Streets 1323; Summers County record; (Rentch et al. 2005).

Danthonia spicata (L.) Beauv. ex Roemer & J. A. Schultes (poverty oatgrass): native; uncommon; Streets 478; Potential Mercer County Record; identified in a vegetation plot during 2003–2006.

Diarrhena americana Beauv. (American beakgrain): native; uncommon; Vanderhorst 7001, 7095, Grafton S.N.

Dichanthelium boscii (Poir.) Gould & C. A. Clark (Bosc's panicgrass): native; common; Streets 448, 476; identified in a vegetation plot during 2003–2006; (Rentch et al. 2005).

Dichanthelium clandestinum (L.) Gould (deertongue): native; common; Streets 566, 633; identified in a vegetation plot during 2003–2006; (Rentch et al. 2005).

Dichanthelium commutatum (J. A. Schultes) Gould ssp. *ashei* (T.G. Pearson ex Ashei) Freckmann & Lelong (variable panicgrass): native; uncommon; Streets 502, 508, 1385, 1393; identified in a vegetation plot during 2003–2006.

Dichanthelium commutatum (J. A. Schultes) Gould ssp. *commutatum* (variable panicgrass): native; common; Streets 574, 591, 745; identified in a vegetation plot during 2003–2006.

Dichanthelium depauperatum (Muhl.) Gould (starved panicgrass): native; uncommon; Streets 474, 501, 586, 752, 1389; Mercer County record; identified in a vegetation plot during 2003–2006.

Dichanthelium dichotomum (L.) Gould (cypress panicgrass): native; unknown abundance; (Rentch et al. 2005).

Dichanthelium dichotomum (L.) Gould ssp. *dichotomum* (cypress panicgrass): native; common; Streets 544, 685, 727, Vanderhorst 6771; identified in a vegetation plot during 2003–2006.

Dichanthelium dichotomum (L.) Gould ssp. *microcarpon* (Muhl. ex Elliott) Freckmann & Lelong (cypress panicgrass): native; uncommon; identified in a vegetation plot during 2003–2006.

Dichanthelium dichotomum (L.) Gould ssp. yadkinense (Ashe) Freckmann & Lelong (cypress panicgrass): native; uncommon; Streets 495, 753, Vanderhorst 7084; identified in a vegetation plot during 2003–2006.

Echinochloa crus-galli (L.) Beauv. (barnyardgrass): native; common; Streets 661, Vanderhorst 7043; identified in a vegetation plot during 2003–2006.

Elymus canadensis L. (Canada wildrye): native; uncommon; Streets 632; Mercer County record; identified in a vegetation plot during 2003–2006.

Elymus hystrix L. var. *hystrix* (eastern bottlebrush grass): native; common; Streets 607; identified in a vegetation plot during 2003–2006.

Elymus riparius Wieg. (riverbank wildrye): native; common; Streets 721, Vanderhorst 6798, 6970, 6979b, 6979c, Grafton S.N.; identified in a vegetation plot during 2003–2006.

Elymus virginicus L. var. *virginicus* (Virginia wildrye): native; uncommon; Vanderhorst 6979A; identified in a vegetation plot during 2003–2006.

Eragrostis hypnoides (Lam.) B. S. P. (teal lovegrass): native; uncommon; Vanderhorst 6968; identified in a vegetation plot during 2003–2006.

Festuca subverticillata (Pers.) Alexeev (nodding fescue): native; common; Streets 428, 1286, Grafton S.N.; identified in a vegetation plot during 2003–2006.

Glyceria striata (Lam.) A. S. Hitchc. (fowl mannagrass): native; common; Streets 510, Vanderhorst 6923; identified in a vegetation plot during 2003–2006.

Holcus lanatus L. (common velvetgrass): exotic; invasive, severe threat; common; Streets 537; identified in a vegetation plot during 2003–2006.

Leersia virginica Willd. (whitegrass): native; uncommon; Streets 648b, 707, 1429; identified in a vegetation plot during 2003–2006.

Lolium arundinaceum (Schreb.) S. J. Darbyshire (tall fescue): exotic; invasive, severe threat; common; Streets 416a, 558; identified in a vegetation plot during 2003–2006.

Lolium pratense (Huds.) S. J. Darbyshire (meadow fescue): exotic; invasive, significant threat; common; identified in a vegetation plot during 2003–2006.

Muhlenbergia sylvaticum Torr. ex Gray (woodland muhly): native; uncommon; Short 15, Grafton S.N.; identified in a vegetation plot during 2003–2006; (Rentch et al. 2005).

Muhlenbergia tenuiflora (Willd.) B. S. P. (slimflower muhly): native; uncommon; Vanderhorst 6776, Grafton S.N..

Panicum anceps L. ssp. *anceps* (beaked panicgrass): native; uncommon; Streets 670, Vanderhorst 7004; identified in a vegetation plot during 2003–2006.

Panicum virgatum L. (switchgrass): native; uncommon; Vanderhorst 6997; identified in a vegetation plot during 2003–2006.

Paspalum laeve Michx. (field paspalum): native; uncommon; Streets 716.

Pennisetum glaucum (L.) R. Br. (pearl millet): exotic; uncommon; identified in a vegetation plot during 2003–2006.

Phalaris arundinacea L. (reed canarygrass): native; invasive, severe threat; common; Streets 557, Vanderhorst 657; identified in a vegetation plot during 2003–2006.

Phleum pratense L. (timothy): exotic; invasive, significant threat; common; Streets 564; identified in a vegetation plot during 2003–2006.

Poa alsodes Gray (grove bluegrass): native; common; Streets 529b, 548, 1285, Vanderhorst 6924; identified in a vegetation plot during 2003–2006.

Poa cuspidata Nutt. (early bluegrass): native; uncommon; Streets 393; identified in a vegetation plot during 2003–2006; (Rentch et al. 2005).

Poa pratensis L. ssp. *pratensis* (Kentucky bluegrass): exotic; invasive, severe threat; common; Streets 408, 581; identified in a vegetation plot during 2003–2006.

Poa sylvestris Gray (woodland bluegrass): native; uncommon; Streets 1595, Vanderhorst 6568; identified in a vegetation plot during 2003–2006.

Poa trivialis L. (rough bluegrass): exotic; invasive, severe threat; common; Streets 563, Vanderhorst 6574; identified in a vegetation plot during 2003–2006.

Schizachyrium scoparium (Michx.) Nash var. *scoparium* (little bluestem): native; uncommon; Short 43; identified in a vegetation plot during 2003–2006.

Sphenopholis nitida (Biehler) Scribn. (shiny wedgescale): native; uncommon; Streets 434, 477, 480, 519, 543, Vanderhorst 6561; identified in a vegetation plot during 2003–2006.

Tridens flavus (L.) A. S. Hitchc. var. *flavus* (purpletop tridens): native; common; Vanderhorst 6792, Short 69.

Polemoniaceae

Phlox divaricata L. (wild blue phlox): native; common; Streets 378.

Phlox maculata L. ssp. *pyramidalis* (Sm.) Wherry (wild sweetwilliam): native; uncommon; Streets 635; identified in a vegetation plot during 2003–2006.

Phlox paniculata L. (fall phlox): native; uncommon; Vanderhorst 7005, Oxley 1191; (Oxley 1975).

Phlox stolonifera Sims (creeping phlox): native; common; Streets 1654, Oxley 1190; identified in a vegetation plot during 2003–2006; (Oxley 1975).

Phlox subulata L. (moss phlox): native; uncommon; Oxley 1189m; identified in a vegetation plot during 2003–2006; (Oxley 1975).

Polygalaceae

Polygala paucifolia Willd. (gaywings): native; uncommon; Streets 1635, Oxley 955; identified in a vegetation plot during 2003–2006; (Oxley 1975).

Polygala senega L. (Seneca snakeroot): native; unknown abundance; Oxley 955; (Oxley 1975).

Polygala verticillata L. (whorled milkwort): native; uncommon; Vanderhorst 6769.

Polygonaceae

Polygonum caespitosum Blume var. *longisetum* (de Bruyn) A. N. Steward (Oriental ladysthumb): exotic; invasive, severe threat; common; Streets 648a, 687,725, 735, Vanderhorst 6753, 6989; identified in a vegetation plot during 2003–2006.

Polygonum convolvulus L. var. *convolvulus* (black bindweed): exotic; invasive, significant threat; uncommon; Potential Summers County record; identified in a vegetation plot during 2003–2006.

Polygonum cuspidatum Sieb. & Zucc. (Japanese knotweed): exotic; invasive, severe threat; uncommon; identified in a vegetation plot during 2003–2006.

Polygonum hydropiperoides Michx. (swamp smartweed): native; uncommon; Streets 1363, Vanderhorst 6990; identified in a vegetation plot during 2003–2006.

Polygonum pensylvanicum L. (Pennsylvania smartweed): native; uncommon; Streets 734, Vanderhorst 6993; identified in a vegetation plot during 2003–2006.

Polygonum persicaria L. (spotted ladysthumb): exotic; invasive, significant threat; unknown abundance; (Oxley 1975).

Polygonum punctatum Ell. (dotted smartweed): native; uncommon; identified in a vegetation plot during 2003–2006.

Polygonum punctatum Ell. var. *punctatum* (dotted smartweed): native; uncommon; Streets 705, 722; identified in a vegetation plot during 2003–2006.

Polygonum sagittatum L. (arrowleaf tearthumb): native; uncommon; Vanderhorst 6797; Potential Summers County record; identified in a vegetation plot during 2003–2006; (Oxley 1975).

Polygonum scandens L. (climbing false buckwheat): unknown origin; uncommon; identified in a vegetation plot during 2003–2006; (Oxley 1975).

Polygonum scandens L. var. *cristatum* (Engelm. & Gray) Gleason (climbing false buckwheat): native; uncommon; Vanderhorst 6754, 7050, 7093, Short 56; Mercer County record; identified in a vegetation plot during 2003–2006.

Polygonum virginianum L. (jumpseed): native; common; Streets 679, Vanderhorst 6799; identified in a vegetation plot during 2003–2006; (Oxley 1975).

Rumex acetosella L. (common sheep sorrel): exotic; invasive, severe threat; common; Oxley 571; identified in a vegetation plot during 2003–2006; (Oxley 1975).

Rumex crispus L. ssp. *crispus* (curly dock): exotic; invasive, significant threat; common; Streets 520, 1336; identified in a vegetation plot during 2003–2006; (Oxley 1975).

Rumex obtusifolius L. (bitter dock): exotic; invasive, watch list; uncommon; Streets 1335; identified in a vegetation plot during 2003–2006; (Oxley 1975).

Portulacaceae

Claytonia caroliniana Michx. (Carolina springbeauty): native; common; Streets 348; (Oxley 1975).

Claytonia virginica L. (Virginia springbeauty): native; common; Streets 333, 391; identified in a vegetation plot during 2003–2006.

Primulaceae

Dodecatheon meadia L. ssp. *meadia* (pride of Ohio): native; uncommon; Streets 398; identified in a vegetation plot during 2003–2006.

Lysimachia ciliata L. (fringed loosestrife): native; common; Streets 750, 1378, Peeke S.N.; identified in a vegetation plot during 2003–2006.

Lysimachia japonica Thunb. (Japanese yellow loosestrife): exotic; common; Streets 528; identified in a vegetation plot during 2003–2006.

Lysimachia nummularia L. (creeping jenny): exotic; invasive, severe threat; common; Streets 535; Potential Mercer County Record; identified in a vegetation plot during 2003–2006.

Lysimachia quadrifolia L. (whorled yellow loosestrife): native; common; identified in a vegetation plot during 2003–2006.

Lysimachia tonsa (Wood) Wood ex Pax & R. Knuth (southern yellow loosestrife): native; unknown abundance; WVNHP tracked, SH, G4; (Oxley 1975).

Pyrolaceae

Chimaphila maculata (L.) Pursh (striped prince's pine): native; uncommon; Streets 506, 582, 1333b; identified in a vegetation plot during 2003–2006; (Oxley 1975, Rentch et al. 2005).

Chimaphila umbellata (L.) W. Bart. ssp. *cisatlantica*(Blake) Hultén (pipsissewa): native; unknown abundance; (Oxley 1975).

Ranunculaceae

Actaea pachypoda Ell. (white baneberry): native; rare; (Oxley 1975).

Actaea racemosa L. var. *racemosa* (black bugbane): native; uncommon; Streets 690, 1321; identified in a vegetation plot during 2003–2006; (Rentch et al. 2005).

Anemone canadensis L. (Canadian anemone): native; unknown abundance; WVNHP tracked, S1, G5; (Norris 1992).

Anemone lancifolia Pursh (mountain thimbleweed): native; uncommon; Streets 1649; Summers County record.

Anemone quinquefolia L. var. *minima* (DC.) Frodin (nightcaps): native; rare; WVNHP tracked, S2, G5T3; Streets 1659; Summers County record.

Anemone quinquefolia L. var. *quinquefolia* (nightcaps): native; uncommon; identified in a vegetation plot during 2003–2006.

Anemone virginiana L. var. *virginiana* (tall thimbleweed): native; common; Short 59.

Aquilegia canadensis L. (red columbine): native; common; Streets 487, 1276; identified in a vegetation plot during 2003–2006; (Oxley 1975).

Clematis virginiana L. (devil's darning needles): native; common; Streets 732, Short 65; Potential Mercer County Record; identified in a vegetation plot during 2003–2006; (Oxley 1975).

Hepatica nobilis Schreb. var. *acuta* (Pursh) Steyermark (sharplobe hepatica): native; uncommon; Streets 320; identified in a vegetation plot during 2003–2006; (Oxley 1975, Norris 1992).

Hepatica nobilis Schreb. var. *obtusa* (Pursh) Steyermark (roundlobe hepatica): native; uncommon; Streets 1433, 1627; identified in a vegetation plot during 2003–2006.

Hydrastis canadensis L. (goldenseal): native; uncommon; Streets 1614, Short 62; (Oxley 1975).

Ranunculus abortivus L. (littleleaf buttercup): native; common; Streets 423; identified in a vegetation plot during 2003–2006.

Ranunculus allegheniensis Britt. (Allegheny Mountain buttercup): nativee; unknown abundance; (Oxley 1975).

Ranunculus fascicularis Muhl. ex Bigelow (early buttercup): native; rare; Vanderhorst 6903; Summers County record; identified in a vegetation plot during 2003–2006.

Ranunculus hispidus Michx. var. *hispidus* (bristly buttercup): native; uncommon; Streets 399.

Ranunculus hispidus Michx. var. *nitidus* (Chapman) T. Duncan (bristly buttercup): native; uncommon; Streets 420; identified in a vegetation plot during 2003–2006.

Ranunculus recurvatus Poir. var. *recurvatus* (blisterwort): native; common; Streets 419, 455, 1277, Oxley 652; identified in a vegetation plot during 2003–2006; (Oxley 1975, Rentch et al. 2005).

Thalictrum dioicum L. (early meadow-rue): native; common; Streets 340, 1658, Tosh S.N.; identified in a vegetation plot during 2003–2006; (Rentch et al. 2005).

Thalictrum pubescens Pursh (king of the meadow): native; uncommon; Streets 1350; (Oxley 1975).

Thalictrum thalictroides (L.) Eames & Boivin (rue anemone): native; common; identified in a vegetation plot during 2003–2006; (Oxley 1975).

Trautvetteria caroliniensis (Walt.) Vail var. *caroliniensis* (Carolina bugbane): native; uncommon; identified in a vegetation plot during 2003–2006.

Rhamnaceae

Ceanothus americanus L. (New Jersey tea): native; uncommon; Streets 1578; identified in a vegetation plot during 2003–2006.

Rosaceae

Agrimonia microcarpa Wallr. (smallfruit agrimony): native; rare; WVNHP tracked, S1, G5; (Norris 1992).

Agrimonia parviflora Ait. (harvestlice): native; uncommon; Streets 748, Vanderhorst 6977; identified in a vegetation plot during 2003–2006.

Agrimonia pubescens Wallr. (soft agrimony): native; common; Streets 641, 704, 1371, 1383; identified in a vegetation plot during 2003–2006.

Agrimonia rostellata Wallr. (beaked agrimony): native; uncommon; Potential Summers County record; identified in a vegetation plot during 2003–2006.

Agrimonia striata Michx. (roadside agrimony): native; uncommon; identified in a vegetation plot during 2003–2006.

Amelanchier arborea (Michx. f.) Fern. var. *arborea* (common serviceberry): native; common; identified in a vegetation plot during 2003–2006; (Oxley 1975, Norris 1992, Rentch et al. 2005).

Amelanchier laevis Wieg. (Allegheny serviceberry): native; unknown abundance; (Oxley 1975).

Aruncus dioicus (Walt.) Fern. (bride's feathers): native; unknown abundance; (Oxley 1975)

Chaenomeles japonica (Thunb.) Lindl. ex Spach (Maule's quince): exotic; uncommon; Streets 346.

Crataegus crus-galli L. (cockspur hawthorn): native; uncommon; Streets 1596; identified in a vegetation plot during 2003–2006.

Crataegus intricata Lange (Copenhagen hawthorn): native; unknown abundance; Oxley 772; (Oxley 1975).

Fragaria virginiana Duchesne ssp. *virginiana* (Virginia strawberry): native; unknown abundance; Oxley 802; (Oxley 1975).

Geum canadense Jacq. var. *canadense* (white avens): native; common; Streets 625, 739; identified in a vegetation plot during 2003–2006.

Geum vernum (Raf.) Torr. & Gray (spring avens): native; common; Streets 425, 1278, Vanderhorst 6918; identified in a vegetation plot during 2003–2006.

Malus coronaria (L.) P. Mill. var. *coronaria* (sweet crabapple): native; common; Grafton S.N.; identified in a vegetation plot during 2003–2006.

Physocarpus opulifolius (L.) Maxim. var. *opulifolius* (common ninebark): native; common; identified in a vegetation plot during 2003–2006; (Oxley 1975, Norris 1992).

Porteranthus trifoliatus (L.) Britt. (Bowman's root): native; unknown abundance; Oxley 757; (Oxley 1975).

Potentilla canadensis L. var. *canadensis* (dwarf cinquefoil): native; common; Streets 400, Vanderhorst 6821; identified in a vegetation plot during 2003–2006.

Potentilla simplex Michx. (common cinquefoil): native; common; Streets 426; identified in a vegetation plot during 2003–2006; (Oxley 1975, Rentch et al. 2005).

Prunus alleghaniensis Porter var. *alleghaniensis* (Allegheny plum): native; unknown abundance; WVNHP tracked, S3, G4T4; Grafton S.N.; (Norris 1992).

Prunus americana Marsh. (American plum): native; uncommon; Streets 737, 1634; identified in a vegetation plot during 2003–2006; (Oxley 1975).

Prunus persica (L.) Batsch (peach): exotic; uncommon; (Oxley 1975).

Prunus serotina Ehrh. var. *serotina* (black cherry): native; abundant; Streets 1641; identified in a vegetation plot during 2003–2006; (Oxley 1975, Norris 1992, Rentch et al. 2005).

Pyrus pyrifolia (Burm. f.) Nakai (Chinese pear): exotic; uncommon; Vanderhorst 6908, 7153; Summers County record; identified in a vegetation plot during 2003–2006.

Rosa carolina L. var. *carolina* (Carolina rose): native; common; Streets 1396; identified in a vegetation plot during 2003–2006; (Oxley 1975).

Rosa multiflora Thunb. ex Murr. (multiflora rose): exotic; invasive, severe threat; abundant; Streets 458; identified in a vegetation plot during 2003–2006; (Oxley 1975, Norris 1992).

Rosa palustris Marsh. (swamp rose): native; uncommon; Streets 523.

Rubus allegheniensis Porter (Allegheny blackberry): native; unknown abundance; (Oxley 1975).

Rubus flagellaris Willd. (northern dewberry): native; uncommon; Streets 1283; identified in a vegetation plot during 2003–2006; (Oxley 1975).

Rubus occidentalis L. (black raspberry): native; common; identified in a vegetation plot during 2003–2006; (Oxley 1975).

Rubus odoratus L. var. *odoratus* (purpleflowering raspberry): native; common; Streets 1326, 1427, Short 37, Oxley 820; identified in a vegetation plot during 2003–2006; (Oxley 1975).

Rubus pensilvanicus Poir. (Pennsylvania blackberry): native; uncommon; Streets 464; Summers County record.

Rubus phoenicolasius Maxim. (wine raspberry): exotic; invasive, severe threat; common; Streets 1639; identified in a vegetation plot during 2003–2006; (Oxley 1975).

Spiraea japonica L. f. var. *fortunei* (Planch.) Rehd. (fortune meadowsweet): exotic; invasive, severe threat; unknown abundance; (Norris 1992).

Spiraea virginiana Britt. (Virginia meadowsweet): native; rare; WVNHP tracked, S1, G2, LT; Streets 1434, Wiebolt S.N.; identified in a vegetation plot during 2003–2006; (Norris 1992).

Waldsteinia fragarioides (Michx.) Tratt. ssp. *fragarioides* (Appalachian barren strawberry): native; unknown abundance; (Oxley 1975).

Rubiaceae

Cephalanthus occidentalis L. (common buttonbush): native; common; Streets 653b, 1360; identified in a vegetation plot during 2003–2006; (Norris 1992).

Galium aparine L. (stickywilly): native; uncommon; Streets 471; identified in a vegetation plot during 2003–2006; (Oxley 1975, Rentch et al. 2005).

Galium asprellum Michx. (rough bedstraw): native; uncommon; identified in a vegetation plot during 2003–2006.

Galium circaezans Michx. (licorice bedstraw): native; common; (Rentch et al. 2005).

Galium circaezans Michx. var. *circaezans* (licorice bedstraw): native; common; Streets 512, 1331, 1580; identified in a vegetation plot during 2003–2006.

Galium circaezans Michx. var. *hypomalacum* Fern. (licorice bedstraw): native; common; Streets 1309; identified in a vegetation plot during 2003–2006.

Galium lanceolatum Torr. (lanceleaf wild licorice): native; common; Streets 1313, Vanderhorst 7052, Short 40; identified in a vegetation plot during 2003–2006.

Galium latifolium Michx. (purple bedstraw): native; uncommon; identified in a vegetation plot during 2003–2006.

Galium triflorum Michx. (fragrant bedstraw): native; abundant; Streets 1310, 1317, 1373; identified in a vegetation plot during 2003–2006; (Rentch et al. 2005).

Houstonia caerulea L. (azure bluet): native; uncommon; Streets 461; identified in a vegetation plot during 2003–2006; (Oxley 1975).

Houstonia longifolia Gaertn. (longleaf summer bluet): native; common; Streets 437, 451, Peeke S.N.; identified in a vegetation plot during 2003–2006; (Oxley 1975, Rentch et al. 2005).

Mitchella repens L. (partridgeberry): native; common; Streets 1445; identified in a vegetation plot during 2003–2006; (Oxley 1975).

Salicaceae

Populus grandidentata Michx. (bigtooth aspen): native; uncommon; Streets 1293c; (Rentch et al. 2005).

Salix caroliniana Michx. (coastal plain willow): native; uncommon; Streets 1572; identified in a vegetation plot during 2003–2006.

Salix nigra Marsh. (black willow): native; uncommon; Streets 1581, 1582, 1660; identified in a vegetation plot during 2003–2006; (Oxley 1975, Norris 1992).

Salix sericea Marsh. (silky willow): native; uncommon; identified in a vegetation plot during 2003–2006.

Santalaceae

Pyrularia pubera Michx. (buffalo nut): native; uncommon; Streets 1366; identified in a vegetation plot during 2003–2006; (Oxley 1975).

Saxifragaceae

Heuchera americana L. (American alumroot): native; unknown abundance; Oxley 742; (Oxley 1975).

Heuchera americana L. var. *americana* (American alumroot): native; uncommon; identified in a vegetation plot during 2003–2006.

Heuchera pubescens Pursh (downy alumroot): native; uncommon; Streets 446, 578, Vanderhorst 7060; Mercer County record, Summers County record; identified in a vegetation plot during 2003–2006.

Heuchera villosa Michx. var. *villosa* (hairy alumroot): native; uncommon; Streets 1442, Vanderhorst 6617; identified in a vegetation plot during 2003–2006.

Mitella diphylla L. (twoleaf miterwort): native; uncommon; Streets 349, 1620; identified in a vegetation plot during 2003–2006; (Oxley 1975).

Saxifraga virginiensis Michx. var. *virginiensis* (early saxifrage): native; uncommon; Streets 334; (Oxley 1975).

Tiarella cordifolia L. (heartleaf foamflower): native; uncommon; Streets 357, Vanderhorst 6827; identified in a vegetation plot during 2003–2006; (Oxley 1975, Norris 1992).

Scrophulariaceae

Aureolaria flava (L.) Farw. var. *flava* (smooth yellow false foxglove): native; uncommon; Vanderhorst 7057; identified in a vegetation plot during 2003–2006.

Aureolaria flava (L.) Farw. var. *macrantha* Pennell (smooth yellow false foxglove): native; uncommon; Streets 1416, 1420; Summers County record; identified in a vegetation plot during 2003–2006.

Aureolaria virginica (L.) Pennell (downy yellow false foxglove): native; uncommon; Grafton S.N.; identified in a vegetation plot during 2003–2006.

Chelone glabra L. (white turtlehead): native; common; identified in a vegetation plot during 2003–2006; (Oxley 1975).

Lindernia dubia (L.) Pennell var. *dubia* (yellowseed false pimpernel): native; uncommon; Streets 660, 1409, Vanderhorst 6969; identified in a vegetation plot during 2003–2006.

Mimulus alatus Ait. (sharpwing monkeyflower): native; uncommon; Streets 659, Unknown collector S.N.; identified in a vegetation plot during 2003–2006.

Mimulus ringens L. var. *ringens* (Allegheny monkeyflower): native; uncommon; Streets 1376; Summers County record; identified in a vegetation plot during 2003–2006.

Paulownia tomentosa (Thunb.) Sieb. & Zucc. ex Steud. (princesstree): exotic; invasive, significant threat; uncommon; Streets 1355; identified in a vegetation plot during 2003–2006.

Pedicularis canadensis L. ssp. *canadensis* (Canadian lousewort): native; uncommon; Streets 1294; (Oxley 1975).

Penstemon canescens (Britt.) Britt. (eastern gray beardtongue): native; common; Streets 447; identified in a vegetation plot during 2003–2006.

Penstemon hirsutus (L.) Willd. (hairy beardtongue): native; uncommon; Streets 1395; Summers County record; identified in a vegetation plot during 2003–2006.

Penstemon pallidus Small (pale beardtongue): native; uncommon; Streets 436; Potential Mercer County Record; identified in a vegetation plot during 2003–2006.

Scrophularia lanceolata Pursh (lanceleaf figwort): native; unknown abundance; Grafton S.N.

Verbascum blattaria L. (moth mullein): exotic; invasive, watch list; uncommon; Streets 550, Oxley 1264m; (Oxley 1975).

Verbascum thapsus L. (common mullein): exotic; invasive, significant threat; common; Oxley 1264; identified in a vegetation plot during 2003–2006; (Oxley 1975).

Veronica americana Schwein. ex Benth. (American speedwell): native; common; identified in a vegetation plot during 2003–2006; (Oxley 1975).

Veronica arvensis L. (corn speedwell): exotic; invasive, significant threat; common; Streets 1288; identified in a vegetation plot during 2003–2006.

Veronica officinalis L. var. *officinalis* (common gypsyweed): exotic; invasive, significant threat; common; Streets 438, 468; (Oxley 1975).

Veronica serpyllifolia L. ssp. *serpyllifolia* (thymeleaf speedwell): exotic; invasive, significant threat; common; Streets 388, Oxley 1283; (Oxley 1975).

Veronicastrum virginicum (L.) Farw. (Culver's root): native; uncommon; Streets 656, Vanderhorst 6995; identified in a vegetation plot during 2003–2006.

Smilacaceae

Smilax ecirrata (Engelm. ex Kunth) S. Wats. (upright carrionflower): native; common; Potential Summers County record; identified in a vegetation plot during 2003–2006.

Smilax glauca Walt. (cat greenbrier): native; common; identified in a vegetation plot during 2003–2006; (Oxley 1975).

Smilax herbacea L. (smooth carrionflower): native; uncommon; Vanderhorst 7073; Mercer County record; identified in a vegetation plot during 2003–2006.

Smilax rotundifolia L. (roundleaf greenbrier): native; common; Streets 1642, Oxley 449; identified in a vegetation plot during 2003–2006; (Oxley 1975).

Smilax tamnoides L. (bristly greenbrier): native; common; Streets 1308, Vanderhorst 7049; identified in a vegetation plot during 2003–2006.

Solanaceae

Datura stramonium L. (jimsonweed): exotic; unknown abundance; (Oxley 1975).

Physalis heterophylla Nees var. *heterophylla* (clammy groundcherry): native; unknown abundance; Grafton S.N.; (Oxley 1975).

Physalis longifolia Nutt. var. *subglabrata* (Mackenzie & Bush) Cronq. (longleaf groundcherry): native; uncommon; Short 19; identified in a vegetation plot during 2003–2006.

Solanum carolinense L. var. *carolinense* (Carolina horsenettle): native; common; Streets 668, 1338; identified in a vegetation plot during 2003–2006; (Oxley 1975).

Staphyleaceae

Staphylea trifolia L. (American bladdernut): native; common; Streets 361b, Vanderhorst 6787; identified in a vegetation plot during 2003–2006; (Norris 1992).

Thymelaeaceae

Dirca palustris L. (eastern leatherwood): native; uncommon; Streets 1579, 1647, Vanderhorst 6608; identified in a vegetation plot during 2003–2006; (Norris 1992).

Tiliaceae

Tilia americana L. (American basswood): native; common; identified in a vegetation plot during 2003–2006; (Rentch et al. 2005).

Tilia americana L. var. *americana* (American basswood): native; common; Streets 1616, 1636.

Typhaceae

Typha latifolia L. (broadleaf cattail): native; unknown abundance; (Oxley 1975).

Ulmaceae

Celtis occidentalis L. (common hackberry): native; common; Streets 504, Streets 1284; identified in a vegetation plot during 2003–2006.

Ulmus americana L. (American elm): native; common; Streets 341, 404; Potential Mercer County Record; identified in a vegetation plot during 2003–2006; (Oxley 1975).

Ulmus rubra Muhl. (slippery elm): native; common; identified in a vegetation plot during 2003–2006; (Oxley 1975, Rentch et al. 2005).

Urticaceae

Boehmeria cylindrica (L.) Sw. (smallspike false nettle): native; uncommon; Streets 663, 708; Potential Mercer County Record; identified in a vegetation plot during 2003–2006; (Oxley 1975).

Laportea canadensis (L.) Weddell (Canadian woodnettle): native; uncommon; Streets 1328; identified in a vegetation plot during 2003–2006; (Rentch et al. 2005).

Pilea pumila (L.) Gray var. *pumila* (Canadian clearweed): native; common; Streets 706; identified in a vegetation plot during 2003–2006; (Rentch et al. 2005).

Urtica dioica L. ssp. *dioica* (stinging nettle): exotic; common; Streets 1334, Grafton S.N.; identified in a vegetation plot during 2003–2006; (Oxley 1975).

Urtica dioica L. ssp. *gracilis* (Ait.) Seland. (California nettle): native; unknown abundance; (Oxley 1975).

Verbenaceae

Phryma leptostachya L. (American lopseed): native; uncommon; Streets 1370; Summers County record, Potential Mercer County Record; identified in a vegetation plot during 2003–2006.

Verbena urticifolia L. var. *urticifolia* (white vervain): native; common; Streets 619, 643, 757; identified in a vegetation plot during 2003–2006.

Violaceae

Hybanthus concolor (T. F. Forst.) Spreng. (eastern greenviolet): native; common; Streets 1652, Grafton S.N.

Viola ×*palmata* L. (early blue violet): native; uncommon; Streets 396, 1624; Mercer County record, Summers County record; identified in a vegetation plot during 2003–2006.

Viola blanda Willd. (sweet white violet): native; unknown abundance; (Rentch et al. 2005).

Viola blanda Willd. var. *blanda* (sweet white violet): native; uncommon; Streets 373.

Viola canadensis L. (Canadian white violet): native; common; Streets 599; identified in a vegetation plot during 2003–2006.

Viola cucullata Ait. (marsh blue violet): native; common; Streets 402; identified in a vegetation plot during 2003–2006.

Viola hastata Michx. (halberdleaf yellow violet): native; common; Streets 345a; identified in a vegetation plot during 2003–2006.

Viola hirsutula Brainerd (southern woodland violet): native; uncommon; Streets 1626.

Viola labradorica Schrank (alpine violet): native; unknown abundance; Grafton S.N.

Viola pubescens Ait. var. *pubescens* (downy yellow violet): native; common; identified in a vegetation plot during 2003–2006.

Viola pubescens Ait. var. *scabriuscula* Schwein. ex Torr. & Gray (downy yellow violet): native; common; Streets 354, 1617, Vanderhorst 6825.

Viola rostrata Pursh (longspur violet): native; uncommon; Streets 358, Vanderhorst 6816, 6826, Peeke S.N.

Viola rotundifolia Michx. (roundleaf yellow violet): native; common; (Rentch et al. 2005).

Viola sagittata Ait. (arrowleaf violet): native; common; (Rentch et al. 2005).

Viola sororia Willd. (common blue violet): native; common; Streets 326, 336; identified in a vegetation plot during 2003–2006; (Rentch et al. 2005).

Viola striata Ait. (striped cream violet): native; common; Streets 369, 384, 1289; identified in a vegetation plot during 2003–2006.

Vitaceae

Ampelopsis arborea (L.) Koehne (peppervine): introduced; uncommon; Potential Summers County record; identified in a vegetation plot during 2003–2006.

Parthenocissus quinquefolia (L.) Planch. (Virginia creeper): native; abundant; Streets 1650; identified in a vegetation plot during 2003–2006; (Norris 1992, Rentch et al. 2005).

Vitis aestivalis Michx. var. *bicolor* Deam (summer grape): native; common; identified in a vegetation plot during 2003–2006.

Vitis riparia Michx. (riverbank grape): native; uncommon; Short 17A; identified in a vegetation plot during 2003–2006.

Vitis rupestris Scheele (sand grape): native; rare; WVNHP tracked, S2, G3; Streets 736b, Vanderhorst 6994; Summers County record; identified in a vegetation plot during 2003–2006.

Vitis vulpina L. (frost grape): native; uncommon; Vanderhorst 6932, 6933, Short 67; identified in a vegetation plot during 2003–2006.

Appendix C. Definitions of plant nativity status.

Nativity	Definition
Native	Plants that occurred in West Virginia prior to European settlement.
Adventive	Plants that are native to North America prior to European settlement, but are not native to West Virginia nor were they introduced, and are now found growing in the state.
Introduced	Plants that are native to North America, have been intentionally introduced in West Virginia, and now have escaped cultivation.
Exotic	Plants that are not native to North America but occur without cultivation.

Appendix D. Definitions of invasive ranks.

Invasive status	Definition
Severe threat	Invasive plant species or ecotypes which posses invasive characteristics, and spread easily into native plant communities and displace native vegetation in West Virginia. This includes species which are or likely could become widespread in West Virginia.
Significant threat	Invasive plant species or ecotypes which possess invasive characteristics, but have less threatening impact on native plant communities in West Virginia. This list includes species which may have the capacity to invade natural communities along disturbance corridors, or to spread from stands in disturbed sites into undisturbed areas, but have fewer characteristics of invasive plant species than those within the Severe threat category.
Lesser threat	Invasive plant species or ecotypes which seem principally spread vegetatively in disturbed areas. These species remain in disturbed corridors, not readily invading natural areas, but occasionally are found to be competitive with disturbance-dependant rare species. This also includes some agricultural weeds.
Watch list	Invasive plant species or ecotypes reported to be problematic elsewhere, but for which we have little credible evidence of their threat to natural areas in West Virginia. Species on this list should be investigated for potential threat to natural vegetation.

Appendix E. Definitions of estimated abundance ranks.

Abundance	Definition
Abundant	Large number of individuals; wide ecological amplitude or occurring in habitats covering a large portion of the park.
Common	Large numbers of individuals predictably occurring in commonly encountered habitats but not those covering a large portion of the park.
Uncommon	Few to moderate numbers of individuals; occurring either sporadically in commonly encountered habitats or in uncommon habitats.
Rare	Few individuals usually restricted to small areas of rare habitat.
Unknown	Abundance unknown.

As the nation's primary conservation agency, the Department of the Interior has responsibility for most of our nationally owned public land and natural resources. This includes fostering sound use of our land and water resources; protecting our fish, wildlife, and biological diversity; preserving the environmental and cultural values of our national parks and historical places; and providing for the enjoyment of life through outdoor recreation. The department assesses our energy and mineral resources and works to ensure that their development is in the best interests of all our people by encouraging stewardship and citizen participation in their care. The department also has a major responsibility for American Indian reservation communities and for people who live in island territories under U.S. administration.

NPS D-009A July 2008